Mental Freedom

Advanced Praise

"Sadly, mental health issues are on the rise. We need solutions, and we need them quickly. With years of experience in the industry, Kim Olver has written a book that humanity needs, *Mental Freedom: You Hold the Key*. I can only hope that people worldwide discover this book and use it. It's a privilege to recommend Mental Freedom."

　–Wendy Nichols

"Mental Freedom is a guiding light that offers insightful approaches in enabling one to traverse through one's inner self-journey of exploration and reverberate in overcoming life's challenges in fulfilling self-actualization."

　–Farida Dsilva Dias, PhD

"Mental Freedom introduced a new paradigm to face everyday life challenges. *Mental Freedom: You Hold the Key* is full of wisdom and techniques that are eye-openers. Everyone can use this book to enrich their life and relationships."

　–Ali Sahebi, PhD

"With Kim Olver's Mental Freedom principles, reintegration becomes a game-changer. It's about breaking free from past limitations and leveling up with unbreakable inner peace, epic resilience, and unstoppable self-confidence."

　–Tony Lamar2

"Kim Olver's *Mental Freedom: You Hold the Key* puts Choice Theory into practice."

　–Hussein Paymozd

"Mental Freedom is a life-changing process for exploring emotional and mental health issues. Kim's approach is excellent. It encapsulates the current scientific information available and gives a user-friendly opportunity to personal growth and freedom!"

–Patrick C. Coughlin, Dip Counselling & Psychotherapy

"Kim Olver's *Mental Freedom: You Hold the Key* provides the guide to finding your true self. Mental Freedom gives you the tools to move your roadblocks out of your way, navigate the potholes of life, and become the best you that you choose to be—the Gift, Learning, Opportunity, and Wisdom of a lifetime."

–Kathy Randolph, LPC

"If your unruly mind is like a wild horse dragging you hither and thither, Kim Olver's *Mental Freedom: You Hold the Key* will teach you how you become a 'mind whisperer' and put you back in the saddle. It'll help you open your heart and reclaim your power. What a blessing!"

–Sue Kranz

"Kim Olver has developed a wonderful, simple platform for assisting individuals to be able to study themselves, to be truly honest, and be able to understand about self-worth, in addition to distinguishing the difference between your Responsibility and Response-Ability and your capability and accountability."

–Jean Still, BHsc-Nursing

"Although I am a psychologist and know different approaches to psychology and I teach or use them in my work, the approach of Mental Freedom is straightforward, fluid, and effective for my clients and me. I got to know this approach in a difficult situation in my life and it helped me to go through a crisis more easily and achieve more peace within me. With her kindness, creativity, and intelligence, Kim has been able to easily and beautifully summarize her work and life experiences in this way, which is valuable and admirable. Don't miss learning about Mental Freedom!"

–Zahra Khoshnevisan, PhD

"*Mental Freedom: You Hold the Key* is a transformative guide that empowers readers to reclaim their inner peace and break free from the shackles of self-doubt. Kim Olver's insightful strategies and compassionate wisdom offer a profound journey towards true mental liberation. In *Mental Freedom: You Hold the Key,* Kim Olver provides an essential masterclass in overcoming life's challenges with confidence and resilience. This empowering program is a beacon of hope for those seeking to navigate the complexities of mental health and achieve lasting Mental Freedom."

–Maryam Yama Gidado

"Kim Olver's Mental Freedom is a platform that can be used with various ethnicities, cultures, and ages. These valuable lessons have been incorporated into my counseling practice, and together, Heroes4Life Consultants uses these dynamic lessons with our military personnel and civilian employees in the training we provide. Participants have stated it has helped them focus on what matters in their life and how they show up for themselves."

–Carmella Navarro

Mental Freedom

You Hold the Key

Book One of the
Mental Freedom™ Series

By Kim Olver

InsideOut Press
PO Box 2666
Country Club Hills, IL 60478

Copyright © 2024 by Kim Olver

All rights reserved. No part of this book may be reproduced in any form on by an electronic or mechanical means, including information storage and retrieval systems, without permission in writing from the publisher, except by a reviewer who may quote brief passages in a review.

First edition July 2024

Cover design by Denise Daub
Interior design by Veronica Daub

For more information about publishing services, please visit www.InsideOutPress.com.

Printed in the United States of America

Library of Congress Control Number: XXXXXX

ISBN-13: 979-8-9852054-3-5

This book is dedicated to everyone who is suffering over something they can't control or change.
My sincere hope is that you will find strategies to relieve your suffering within these pages.

Contents

1. Introduction 1
2. What Motivates You? 13

Open Your Heart

3. Responsibility vs. Response-ability . . . 35
4. The Unconditional Trust Challenge . . . 57

Free Your Mind

5. Empowering vs. Victimizing Language . 77
6. Rewriting the Stores in Your Head 93

Transform Your Life

7. Signals vs. Solutions 117
8. Appreciating the GLOW 139
9. The Head, Heart, and Hands 149

Acknowledgements 155

Foreword

By Teresa Greco

Amidst the hustle and bustle of modern life, finding peace and happiness can feel like an elusive quest, a journey fraught with unexpected obstacles. In the words of Ralph Waldo Emerson, "Nobody can bring you peace but yourself." It is a profound statement that echoes through our minds, reminding us of the inherent power we possess to shape our own realities. This book serves as a guide to a deeply personal journey to reconnect with the core of our being, where love, peace, and happiness reside. Mental Freedom is not merely a philosophical or theoretical ideal; it is a practical path back to the tranquillity and joy that constitute the essence of our true selves.

Echoing Emerson's sentiment, Aristotle postulated that "Happiness is the meaning and the purpose of life, the whole aim and end of human existence." Indeed, the pursuit of happiness lies at the heart of human endeavours, steering our actions and shaping our destinies – whether it be through material possessions, social status, or personal achievements. If you ask yourself why you want the big house, fancy car, prestigious job, social media followers, and designer clothes, is it because you think it'll make you happier?

But where does one find true happiness amidst the complexities of modern life? Science has shown that happiness is not found in our possessions, positions, titles, degrees, relationships, appearances, and experiences, yet many of us have lost ourselves in the misconceptions of the "American Dream." We strive for external successes only to find that they do not fulfill our deepest needs. This misalignment between our external pursuits and internal desires manifests as a persistent sense of emptiness and discontent, a testament to the fact that happiness is not a destination to be reached but an inner journey to be embraced.

Mental Freedom is a program meticulously designed to instill a sense of empowerment in individuals, reminding them that their lives are the only things we can truly control. We cannot control others or external circumstances, only our responses to them. Mental Freedom equips us with practical tools to help ourselves rather than blaming external factors and wishing they were different. People say, "If only you acted more like this or things were less of that, then I'd be happy." This perspective places happiness outside oneself instead of recognizing that joy can be found within at any moment.

When we feel disconnected from our happiness and peace, it signals a misalignment within us. Listening to the communication of our physical, mental, emotional, and spiritual selves can help guide us toward self-discovery and balance. Are your shoulders tense, calling for a stretch? Are your thoughts filled with self-doubt, needing a shift toward self-compassion? Are your emotions in turmoil, seeking calm? You may lack a sense of meaning and purpose, trapped in a cycle of emptiness and inauthenticity. By attuning to these signals, we embark on a journey of self-discovery that promises to bring us back into harmony with the wholeness and health of our being. Mental Freedom offers a structured approach to achieving this balance and realignment, guiding us step by step towards a more fulfilling and joyful life.

Recognizing that you have complete control over your own life, determining its direction through the choices and decisions you make moment by moment, you gain the power to feel that anything is possible. As creators of our own lives, we must align our actions with our true selves, free from the limiting beliefs imposed by individuals around us, such as family, friends, teachers, and religious leaders. These influences shape our perceptions of who we are, what we can achieve, and who we can become, often causing us to relinquish our autonomy from a young age.

Over time, we may forget that we alone can decide the direction our lives will take. Mental Freedom reminds us of our true power and the creative nature of our being. It encourages us to design a life guided by our inner selves rather than being swayed by external influences. Mental Freedom is not only a return to peace but also a return to our true selves. It prompts us to reflect on our needs and values and to make choices that align with them.

When you're armed with the knowledge that can help you be

the captain of your own ship, no one can derail you but yourself. An old proverb wisely states, "You can't tame the wind, but you can turn your sail." Many of us attempt to control external forces, only to find they are far more unyielding and powerful than we are. Instead, we should focus on "turning our sail" and navigating through life's storms with confidence and resilience. Mental Freedom equips us with the knowledge and tools to steer our own lives, guiding us back to calm waters rather than feeling like victims to the uncontrollable forces around us.

Tools are necessary to navigate the challenges of daily life and address past setbacks. Each day presents its own set of difficulties; whether we are stuck in traffic, having a disagreement with a coworker, or dealing with chaos in our homes, we can be left feeling disarrayed. Many of us are not taught the skills we need to know to bring us back into alignment. Mental Freedom offers these tools, enabling us to confront life's adversities effectively. As a certified life coach, Kim contacted me to partake in the research to prove the efficacy of Mental Freedom. After having completed different coaching certifications, I was intrigued by the fact that she had created a program where participants receive actionable steps to navigate all of life's challenges and return to peace in just six weekly sessions.

During the research phase, Mental Freedom was implemented by practitioners worldwide, from therapists and counsellors to educators and coaches working across diverse settings such as addiction centres, private practices, universities, and correctional facilities. Mental Freedom was proven to be effective in every situation. This fact impressed me greatly as it empowers individuals with concrete strategies to navigate challenges independently or with a certified practitioner if they choose to discuss their issues.

My journey to happiness was one I undertook mainly on my own. I turned to a variety of books, podcasts, courses, and lectures to navigate the emotional scars left by past experiences and relationships. I was uncomfortable sharing my private and personal situations with others, and I love how Mental Freedom offers this privacy to my clients as well. However, as the adage goes, "When the student is ready, the teacher will appear." In my over 10-year journey toward healing, the Universe consistently provided the perfect tools to help me process and work through my painful emotions. This led me to become the founder of Steps to Happiness Coaching, a personal development company that helps individuals and organizations looking for the steps they can take to experience more happiness, love, and peace in their lives. I believe the Mental Freedom program aligns with this mission.

As an educator with over 25 years of experience, I appreciate the psycho-educational delivery format of the program. Each week, participants learn about a specific tool and its tenets, gaining insights on how to apply it to various situations and experiences. The sessions include real-life examples and weekly applications, helping individuals connect the tool to both their personal and professional lives. I was particularly impressed by the simplicity of each tool and yet its ability to comprehensively address the most complex issues. This effectiveness stems from the design of each tool, which targets situations from multiple angles, ensuring no aspect is overlooked. Every week, I eagerly anticipated discovering the next tool that would further empower me to take control of my life.

It is encouraging to know that when I experience negative thoughts and emotions, I now have six tools that I can immediately apply, fostering a proactive approach to maintaining my peace and happiness. Additionally, I can share these six tools with others, helping them navigate situations compromising their Mental Freedom. I recall a client who had issues with her neighbours, and I reminded her to protect her peace. Mental Freedom provides the ability to choose whether to remain in a state of struggle and pain or to take steps to preserve one's peace.

Another client's journey illustrates the profound impact of this program. Haunted by a traumatic past relationship as a teen, Mental Freedom gave her the clarity she needed to heal from that experience. She understood that as a young girl, she did her best with the knowledge she had at the time. She made the choice to forgive herself and the other person and to release the pain she had been holding onto for years. This transformation is an example of the program's power to facilitate deep personal healing and empowerment, which is why I decided to offer the program to my clients. Mental Freedom provides them with a toolkit they can apply to help them work through any blocks to their happiness.

Are you ready to take control of your life and align with your true self? Whether you're seeking to release past traumas, overcome relationship or parenting problems, or cope with life's unfortunate events, Mental Freedom offers the tools and guidance to achieve this. By embracing the principles within this book, you can navigate life's challenges with grace and resilience, reclaim your peace, and live a life of genuine happiness.

In the pages that follow, you will find not only a roadmap to Mental Freedom but also a call to return to the love, peace, and happiness that are your birthright. Let this book be your guide on this transformative journey, empowering you to live a life true to your highest self and unlock the boundless potential that lies within.

Welcome to your journey toward Mental Freedom.

Teresa Greco, B.A., B.Ed., M.Ed, is a certified happiness life coach pursuing her Ph.D. in transpersonal psychology and inner happiness.

She is a multiple-time TEDx speaker, 4X bestselling author, international writer, and editor of a Canadian lifestyle magazine. An educator of over 25 years and educational technologies consultant, Teresa is also the host of two Internet TV and radio shows. As a coach, reiki master, and spiritual guide, she holds workshops and mentors others about embracing, honouring, and loving their true authentic selves and achieving their own personal happiness and fulfillment. **teresagreco.ca**

Introduction

"Emancipate yourselves from mental slavery.
None but ourselves can free our minds." –Bob Marley

Mental Freedom is my rebuttal to our mental health system—a broken thing that sees people as broken things. As someone with more than 40 years of experience helping people face the challenges in their lives, I understand that the ability to free ourselves from everything that is painful comes from within. People are fully capable of managing their problems as the whole and unbroken individuals they are when educated, equipped, and empowered with the right information.

I was exposed to the ideas of William Glasser, MD, in 1987. My new job at a foster care agency required a multiday training in Choice Theory®, Dr. Glasser's explanation of human behavior, and Reality Therapy®, his counseling technique for helping people evaluate whether their behavior is helping or preventing them from getting what they want. At the time, my bachelor's degree in psychology taught me a little about a lot of things. The university I graduated from had encouraged us to be eclectic, but that just made for an experience akin to throwing spaghetti against the wall to see what sticks. The training in Choice Theory provided a logical, meaningful deep dive into understanding human behavior from a new lens. I absolutely loved it, and I especially loved my trainer, Nancy Buck. She was living a life I had only dreamed of, raising her two boys and traveling the country to teach ideas she was so passionate about. I remember thinking to myself, I want to be her when I grow up! Little did I know then how much that training would change my life. What started as an important tool added in my toolbox became something that fully restructured how I saw the world.

Although I implemented this tool in my work with foster children and their families, I didn't use it to improve my own life. I often experienced frustration and expressed it by nagging my husband and yelling at my children. These misery-inducing behaviors would continue for the first seven years of knowing Choice Theory, even when I was certified in 1992 and became faculty in 1993. I was good at teaching it, but I taught from intellectual knowledge, repeating things I knew Glasser, its founder, had said.

When my husband, Dave, got sick with leukemia in 1994, my whole world turned upside down. We weren't sure of the prognosis; a full cure was possible with a good match and a bone marrow transplant. The odds of finding a match were good with his six siblings, but it never materialized, and I never felt more powerless.

During this time, I made a conscious decision to lean into Choice Theory, which teaches you to focus on the things you have control over while accepting the rest. I shifted my energy and attention from everything I couldn't control to the things I could: I ate healthier and lost weight, invested in some work projects, and spent concentrated quality time with my children and husband. We poured energy into fundraising efforts and managed to add 350 people to the bone marrow registry at $100 per person, but still, no match for my husband.

In 1999, Dave went ahead with a mismatched donor transplant from his uncle, a three-out-of-six match. It went well at first, but eventually, he started showing signs of rejection, so his anti-rejection medication was increased. This resulted in the pervasive yeast infection that was listed on his death certificate as the reason for his passing.

My sons were 10 and 8 at the beginning of my husband's illness, and when Dave passed, they were 15 and 13. Suddenly, there I was—a single mom raising two strong-willed, testosterone-filled teenage boys. My husband had served as the disciplinarian in our family. I got to play good cop to his bad cop, but this was ineffective without Dave playing his role. I knew I needed to parent differently but didn't know where to begin—until I remembered Choice Theory.

While I didn't want to parent with the iron first my husband used, I understood I couldn't be as permissive as I had been. Instead, I moved to the middle of the parenting continuum and became more effective as a result. Don't get me wrong—it wasn't perfect parenting by any stretch of the imagination! In fact, it was downright messy, but I was able to rely on a structure that helped me maintain my sanity and kept those boys alive, sometimes by the skin of their teeth.

Just when I thought I had navigated the toughest areas of parenting, my youngest son, Kyle, decided he wanted to join the Army and fight in Iraq. Tackling this was more difficult than learning to be a single parent ever was. It was a week before Kyle's 18th birthday, so he still required my signature to join, but living your life by the concepts of Choice Theory means supporting people even when what they want makes your life harder. Agreeing to provide that signature was excruciatingly painful for me, but I am proud of that parenting decision. Kyle completed two tours in Iraq and became a sergeant before he came home and started his family, and I couldn't be prouder of the man he is today.

Another experience that tested my Choice Theory competency was in 2014 when a hot air balloon accident left me with two broken ankles. I was in the area for work, but I found myself with a free day, so I decided to cross an item off my bucket list. It was an amazing experience until it was time to land.

Some unexpected wind pushed us horizontally toward a mountain, so the pilot tried to lift over it, but equipment failure prevented him from increasing elevation, and there was nowhere else to go but down. We fell much faster than we should have and hit an ironwood tree—the first impact, which broke my right ankle. As the pilot freed us from the tree, another impact broke my left ankle in three places, requiring surgery and some hardware to put back together. Even before I was retrieved from the balloon, I thought to myself, "*Well, Kim, now you have the opportunity to practice what you preach.*" And so I did. I was told I would be in a wheelchair for at least four months, but I was able to walk after two. The doctors had no medical explanation and could only credit my positive attitude. I'll take it!

Even though I learned these concepts in 1987, it wasn't until I faced life-altering challenges beyond my control that I began to truly integrate them into my daily life. Every crisis became an opportunity to lean further into Choice Theory, and now it's hard to tell where Choice Theory leaves off and I begin. Choice Theory is no longer something I teach or something I do; it's who I am.

When Covid-19 invaded the world and threw us into total chaos, I was scared, disorganized, and displaced. I was visiting my mother in Florida when the news broke. I had planned to stay with her until the end of March, but I no longer had to travel to speaking engagements; all my remaining work could be done remotely. I didn't want to leave my mother to cope with this pandemic alone, so I stayed until June. Plus, there was the bonus benefit of getting to spend spring in Florida instead of Chicago.

After two weeks had passed, I recognized I was dwelling in anxiety and fear and thought, "*Kim, what are you doing? You know how to manage this better.*" So, I shifted my focus toward applying Choice Theory to the pandemic experience. I began advertising free support sessions, and for people I knew on Facebook, I hosted Friday evening happy hours on Zoom. People assumed I was doing it to help others, and I was, but those sessions helped me just as much. Not only did I create ways to feel useful, but I also created opportunities for fun during a time when there was little fun to be had. It soon became obvious that I was having a much easier time living through the pandemic than many others I knew. As I started to examine why this was, Mental Freedom was born.

At that point in my career, several different people had already recognized that I wasn't just teaching Choice Theory, I was practicing and living it. Prior to Covid-19, I didn't have much time to consider what that meant, but with all my new free time in 2020, I sat with those observations and thought about what it could mean. I realized Choice Theory had morphed from something I taught into something I practiced, starting as a powerful tool in my toolbox before becoming the whole toolbox. Now, it is the very essence of who I am. I no longer have any idea who I would be without Dr. William Glasser's Choice Theory, and I'm so grateful.

The pandemic gave me time and space for this reflection, allowing me to gather my thoughts about how I was able to fully integrate Choice Theory into my life. Although I learned Choice Theory in 1987, it wasn't until my husband got sick in 1995 that I began to apply it to my personal life, and it wasn't until 2001 that I was fully utilizing it in every aspect of my life. That was a 14-year-long process!

I thought about the many challenges life put in my path, each testing me to apply everything I learned, and my lifelong career of helping others. I realized I was in a unique position to develop a process for introducing the internal control psychology principles that had guided my life for so long—a process that wouldn't take 14 years for people to fully embrace and implement into their own lives.

You may already be familiar with the tenets of Choice Theory developed by Dr. Glasser. While it's built on those concepts, Mental Freedom goes beyond to provide the optimal pathway—a major shortcut to implementing internal control psychology into every aspect of your life. After digesting the information in this book, you won't ever be able to look at life the same way again. I've had many opportunities to see firsthand how powerful and life-changing the concepts were for people after practicing Mental Freedom with some clients and beta groups. (You can find testimonials and reviews at OlverInternational.com/Mental-Freedom.) Considering what the outcomes and preliminary research are showing, I expect Mental Freedom to become an evidence-based practice in short order.

Even though he passed away in 2013, Dr. Glasser continues to be my role model. One thing about following a role model who was still living: His body of work was never done. Every year, he hosted a conference, gathering people from around the world who wanted to learn his latest thoughts on Choice Theory. And believe me, he always had new thoughts. His mind never stopped! Just when you caught up with his thoughts from the year before, he would add and expand on those ideas at the next conference. That was frustrating and exciting in equal measure. I really loved that.

Choice Theory began as Control Theory, a nod to something Dr. Glasser felt perfectly explained why Reality Therapy worked, Perceptual Control Theory, developed by William Powers. For years, instructors at the William Glasser Institute taught Control Theory, even as Dr. Glasser expanded it and developed additional concepts like the five basic human needs and, the one he was most proud of, total behavior. Naming it Choice Theory not only considered these new concepts but also addressed a problem Dr. Glasser had discovered: People believed Control Theory provided methods to control others when it offered the opposite, methods to control oneself. Dr. Glasser encouraged instructors to continue expanding beyond his own concepts, but he wouldn't want them to call it Choice Theory; he wanted them to call it something else. If Glasser were alive and working today, he would have added exponentially to his body of work by now, so I want to honor him by carrying on the essence of his work in Mental Freedom.

I have always wanted to help others, but I didn't always know how. At the beginning of my career, I felt helpful when my clients liked me, wanted to share their personal troubles with me, and *needed* me to help and support them. Now, I believe I'm most effective when I can provide the tools people need to help themselves.

Mental Freedom is the ultimate toolbox for dismantling the misery we create and subconsciously maintain. You may have experienced serious trauma in your life, but that doesn't mean you are broken or destined for a lifetime of unhappiness. It's not just the events in our lives that make us happy or sad; it's our response that contributes to how we experience pain.

Because of this, I believe we create 90% of our own mental and emotional distress—most people just don't realize it, and those who do might not know how to stop it. Enter Mental Freedom, a process that helps people gain control over their state of mind, thus freeing them from any self-created misery they have been carrying around without realizing.

You are a competent person with the capacity to help yourself once you have the information and the willingness to practice using the tools Mental Freedom provides, starting here in this book.

THE RESEARCH

A good friend of mine, Nasrollah Navid, MD, suggested I plan to do some research so I could incorporate that into the book.

I had no idea how to do that. I am a clinician, not a researcher, but I clearly saw value in the idea. I reached out to a researcher I know, Cameron B. Richardson, PhD, from Penn State. He helped me design the research. I trained and certified 23 counselors and coaches from a variety of countries, serving a wide variety of clients, in the Mental Freedom process.

These newly certified Mental Freedom counselors and coaches then worked with half of their clients using the Mental Freedom process and worked with the others using their treatment as usual.

Participants took two pre- and post-assessments: The Ways of Coping Questionnaire and Ryff's Scales of Psychological Well-Being. The research was conducted by Figen Karadogan, PhD, in psychology at Governors State University in University Park, IL. As of the publishing of this book, the data was analyzed on the pre- and post-assessments of Ryff's Scales of Psychological Well-Being. There were significant results for both the Mental Freedom group and the other counseling and coaching groups, evidence that Mental Freedom was shown to be just as significant as other methods. There was not a control group that received no treatment.

There were significant results on the autonomy, environmental mastery, and self-acceptance scales, with marginally significant results on the positive relations and personal growth scales of Riff's Scales of Psychological Well-being. The sample size was 52, so further research will need a control group and a larger sample size. The results of the Ways of Coping Questionnaire have not yet been analyzed. Future questions will be about whether Mental Freedom is more effective as a counseling or coaching approach.

Mental Freedom's OFT Process

It's likely you will encounter concepts that cause you to question this material, but I encourage you to approach it with an open mind. Consider the possibilities: What if what you have believed for most of your life is not correct? What if there are alternative ways to think about things? What if you have more control than you ever thought possible?

In the chapters that follow, you will progress through Mental Freedom's six principles, each revealing methods to Open Your Heart, Free Your Mind, and Transform Your Life—what I like to call Mental Freedom's OFT process.

Open Your Heart: Get along better with the important people in your life.

1. **Responsibility vs. Response-ability:** Your Mental Freedom suffers when you don't take responsibility for the things you are responsible for: your actions, thoughts, needs, decisions, and happiness, in addition to your half of each relationship you share with the people in your life. This translates to not taking responsibility for things other people should be responsible for. Choosing to be response-able is the understanding that you are responsible for how you chose to respond; no one can *make* you do anything.

2. **The Unconditional Trust Challenge:** Your Mental

Freedom decreases when you trust people to match the picture you have of them in your head, which typically involves counting on them to meet your expectations or do exactly what you want them to do. People do not operate that way; they always choose the best way they know how to get what they want in any particular moment. That is the one thing you can trust everyone to do, and when you learn to trust in this way, people don't have the power to disappoint you.

Free Your Mind: Let your mind work for you instead of against you.

3. **Disempowering versus Empowering Language:** You can sacrifice your Mental Freedom not only with your words but also with your thoughts. By eliminating disempowering phrases and replacing them with empowering language, you can reclaim Mental Freedom. Once you can shift from a "have to" to a "want to" mindset, you will never *have* to do anything again!

4. **Rewriting the Stories in Your Head:** Evolution has hardwired our brains for negativity to increase the likelihood of our survival. However, if you have the time to read this book, I will bet that your life is not currently hanging in the balance. Upon encountering unexpected circumstances, you can choose to shift from negative narratives to stories that help you feel better. Either way, the stories we tell ourselves are mostly fabrications, so why not create a positive story when we don't have all the information? When this concept is fully realized, you can drop the need for a narrative completely by embracing each moment as it comes.

Transform Your Life: Learn about understanding and transforming your pain from negative to neutral or even positive.

5. **Pain: Signal versus Solution:** Recognize your pain as a signal that something is amiss and it's time to address it. This problem-solving framework replaces the typical default of blaming others for your pain or ignoring it completely. The default route allows your pain to become the solution for getting something you want, and often, this happens without your awareness.

6. **Appreciating the GLOW:** After learning to distinguish the difference between Signals and Solutions, you can start to appreciate the GLOW—gifts, lessons, opportunities, and wisdom—and transform your pain into something neutral or even positive with practice.

Trigger Warning

There are several times in this book when graphic examples are provided involving death, sexual assault, child sexual abuse, substance use, or suicide.

Mental Freedom has been used successfully with people who have suffered unresolved trauma. However, if you are experiencing serious symptoms from your trauma, it might be helpful for you to first have some IFS, EFT or EMDR sessions, three evidence-based techniques therapists use to treat people who are coping with trauma, to break the connection between the emotions you experience and the actual events of your trauma before continuing with Mental Freedom. Please take care of yourself. If you need to stop reading and come back later, do that. If you need to call someone to support you, do that. Should you need professional attention, please reach out to a counselor who can help.

Summary

1. It is important to know the origin of Mental Freedom and its goals.

2. It's in the early stages, but the preliminary research shows the significant benefits of Mental Freedom in the areas of autonomy, environmental mastery, and self-acceptance. There were marginally significant results in the areas of positive relations and personal growth.

3. The OFT process offers six principles that will expand and enhance the Mental Freedom you experience in your life.

4. People experiencing serious symptoms of trauma may need some IFS, EFT, or EMDR sessions prior to applying Mental Freedom.

5. This book contains a trigger warning.

What Motivates You?

"There is nothing, absolutely nothing, more important than meeting our basic human needs." –Simon Cohen

It's impossible to achieve true Mental Freedom without a solid understanding of who you are, what you want, and the person you want to be.

Who you are is largely determined by the genetic makeup of your basic needs, what you absorbed from your family and culture, the knowledge you've accumulated, and the values you hold. What you want, at any given time, is what you believe will best satisfy your basic needs. Who you want to be refers to the ideal version of yourself you strive for. When you are operating with Mental Freedom, this ideal image you hold of yourself becomes the beacon of light that illuminates the path to get where you want to be without compromising that image. Knowing yourself is key to creating the Mental Freedom you desire.

After discovering your "why" and making the commitment for your Mental Freedom journey, the next step is to understand and build a healthy, loving relationship with yourself. If you haven't yet done this, I recommend setting this book aside and beginning with my book, *Choosing Me Now*, but if you feel satisfied with your progress in this area, read on.

Get to know what motivates you in life. Motivation might seem like something external, but motivation always comes from within. I don't call myself a motivational speaker because I can't motivate anyone other than myself. I prefer to say I am an informational speaker because I provide information that could help motivate you into action, but you are the only one who can motivate yourself.

Choice Theory posits that the strength of these basic needs—Safety & Security, Connection, Significance, Freedom, and Joy—is genetically determined and remains relatively stable over time. But how can we account for those times when one of our lesser-important needs seemed most critical?

According to Dr. William Glasser's Choice Theory psychology, all humans have five basic needs, but we are each genetically programmed at birth to be more strongly motivated by some needs than others. For example, I am most strongly motivated by Connection and Freedom, moderately by Significance, and to a much lesser degree by Safety & Security and Joy.

Context is relevant: There will be times in your life when one of your lower-priority needs takes precedence. If you find yourself in a situation where one of your needs is difficult to satisfy, it will be depleted and become your most vital one, even though its genetically coded strength hasn't changed.

For example, I am hardly ever strongly motivated by Safety & Security, but if I lost my income, had gone through my savings, and couldn't pay my mortgage, I would be extremely motivated by my need for Safety & Security. It hasn't become my highest need, but it takes all my focus because I wouldn't know how to meet it under those circumstances. Both things are motivating—the genetic strength and the situational pressures.

Without contextual pressures, the needs that your DNA dictates are strongest will likely rule the day. However, situational pressures that make it challenging to meet certain needs will cause them to be depleted and become the strongest motivator of your behavior.

Consider yourself and determine which needs were biologically determined to be the strongest for you. As you reflect on the course of your life, do you see a pattern of motivation? Can you pinpoint the needs that have motivated most of your decisions and behaviors throughout your lifetime? That answer would indicate the need or needs that were programmed as your strongest.

A challenging part of Mental Freedom is that until you understand how to check in with yourself and measure these five motivators in each situation, you will feel frustrated or out-of-sorts without understanding why or knowing how to fix it. This can manifest as feeling exhausted regularly, being snippy with the people you care about, having difficulty making decisions, or being unable to truly look at yourself in the mirror.

Basic Human Needs

In Choice Theory, Dr. Glasser called his needs Love & Belonging, Survival, Power, Freedom, and Fun. Unlike Abraham Maslow's more well-known model, the five basic needs as defined by Dr. Glasser are not hierarchal. Maslow posits that these needs build upon each other to ascend from survival to self-actualization whereas Dr. Glasser simply describes things people need in their lives to feel content.

In Mental Freedom, I call the needs Connection, Safety & Security, Significance, Freedom, and Joy. While the names of the needs slightly differ, they are essentially the same, but the terms used in Mental Freedom seem to resonate better than the Choice Theory terms identified in the '70s. I updated the labels for the following reasons:

1. The people interested in studying Mental Freedom would not likely be experiencing challenges to their very survival. If their Survival need was threatened, they would be focused on staying alive rather than achieving Mental Freedom. It's more appropriate that a student of Mental Freedom would be looking for greater safety or security, so we choose to call it Safety & Security instead of referring to it as Survival as Glasser did.

2. I expanded upon Glasser's concept of Love & Belonging by using the term Connection to include connections of all kinds like the environment, animals, a company's mission and values—virtually

anything else you can experience connection with. With the label Love & Belonging, the need is almost always considered to be focused on relationships. Connection encompasses more than that.

3. I changed the term Power to Significance because I believe that the word "power" has taken on a lot of negative connotations since Dr. Glasser developed Choice Theory. Today, when many people hear the word power, they relate it to the bully on the playground, a control freak, or the boss who takes credit for others' work. While those behaviors are ways to meet the need for Significance, they are not exclusively what Glasser meant. In Choice Theory, we talk about three types of Power: power over others, power with others, and power within. Significance eliminates that negative connotation but can still explain bullying behavior, which involves power over others. We all have a need to be significant, to make a difference, and to matter.

4. Freedom in Mental Freedom is exactly what Glasser talked about in Choice Theory: being able to do what you want, when you want, without restriction.

5. I renamed Glasser's term Fun to Joy because many adults believe they no longer have a need for Fun; they've stopped playing in the way they did as a child. However, there is more to Fun than play, and calling it Joy encompasses all aspects of this need.

Choice Theory remains a theory because we have not yet discovered the genes or chromosomes that correspond with each of these needs. Glasser theorized that the five basic needs are genetically programmed and remain relatively stable over time, as evidenced by people being able to pinpoint a lifelong pattern.

Much of my past behavior, including as a small child, was motivated by my desire to be liked by others (Connection), and I often challenged authority with my inability to blindly follow the rules, especially if they didn't make sense to me (Freedom).

Signs you are motivated by Significance include wanting to lead others, be in the spotlight, and work at making an impact in your life. When Safety & Security is foremost, you might feel anxious about doing things spontaneously, make plans to handle anything that could go wrong, and spend time thinking about the future. If Joy is your main motivator, you likely prioritize fun, have a good sense of humor, and enjoy discovering new things. Are you able to notice a pattern of being motivated by one or two of these basic needs throughout your life?

No one's life is shaped by just one need; everyone is driven by a unique combination of all five. Because the other four needs influence you in unique ways, it's rare for one need to perfectly describe you. The five needs interact within each individual in unique ways, and the first step to understanding how yours interact is by determining your individual strength-level profile. To do this, you must learn what motivates you in any given situation.

The way I conceive of this is by imagining the needs as five differently sized buckets to represent the genetically coded strength of each need. Never changing, the size of your buckets stands for how essential each of the needs are to you: The bigger the bucket, the more imperative and motivating the need. For this reason, you will spend much of your time looking for ways to fill your largest buckets until they become full. When this happens, those needs are satisfied, and you will be motivated to attend to the others.

You are happiest when your buckets are full, but not overflowing. The bucket that is most empty will be the one you experience most acutely, propelling you to find ways to satisfy it. As an example, the size of my buckets from largest to smallest is Connection, Freedom, Significance, Joy and Safety & Security. If my Freedom bucket is full, I am at peace with this need and it doesn't motivate my actions. However, imagine my Connection bucket is 50% depleted, my Significance bucket is overflowing, my Safety & Security bucket is perfectly filled, and my Joy bucket is empty. Which one do you think will be motivating me in that moment? If you said Joy, you would be correct.

Living your life reveals a myriad of things that fill your buckets and satisfy your needs. What happens when your containers overflow?

It's entirely possible that you will experience situations when you have more of a need than you want—your container is overflowing. Having more than you need in one area may cause another area to become frustrated since these needs are intricately and intimately connected. In the previous example, my overflowing Significance bucket could be the reason for the 50% depletion in Connection and emptiness in Joy. Inversely, an overflowing Joy bucket could compromise Significance, and having more Connection than I need could cause a depletion in Freedom, and so on.

It is context, the events and circumstances of your life, as well as your developmental stage, that influence just how full your buckets are. You may be feeling content with your life before finding out the company you worked at for 25 years is going out of business and your spouse of 32 years has left you. These circumstances don't change the size of your buckets, but they will dictate how full they are. In this case, the result would likely be an overflowing Freedom bucket that adversely affects all the others.

Without the presence of situational or contextual frustrations, you can typically discern the one or two needs that have consistently been a driving force in your life. The next time you're faced with these situations, you can understand that the need hasn't become more prominent, it is unsatisfied and feels much more pressing, causing feelings like frustration, anxiety, anger, or sadness. This knowledge reveals where you need to focus your efforts to return to contentment—and buckets that are perfectly full.

Trust that you will naturally feel driven to satisfy your depleted basic needs. You may make a conscious decision to forego one need in favor of another during a challenging period in your life, but the five basic needs will refuse the neglect and demand you to address them. Without this understanding, you'll be blindly working toward mending the problem. Not knowing the true motivation behind your actions could cause you to make unhelpful or even damaging decisions. Armed with this knowledge, in addition to responsible and healthy ways to meet the depleted needs, you can strategize from an informed position, potentially avoiding doing something you aren't proud of. For example, let's say you put Joy on the back burner to focus on completing a project, paying off bills, or going to school. It won't be long before you will need to answer the call to experience Joy in your life. Ignoring that call, you may find yourself drinking way too much and being quite obnoxious in the middle of a party where you only intended to make a brief appearance.

As if that weren't complicated enough, what need your behavior satisfies differs from one person to the next. What is experienced as Freedom for one person may be perceived as Significance by someone else. Sex and religion are great examples of this. Sex meets the need for Safety & Security when your goal is to make a baby, which ultimately contributes to the survival of the human species. When loving and respectful feelings are involved, sex can meet the need for Connection. It can serve Significance when it is viewed as a conquest, or if one or both are particularly proud of their partner due to attraction, skills, or even finances. The opportunity for personal expression through sex can satisfy Freedom, and it can also meet the need for Joy through the physical sensations and emotions that come from the act itself.

The same is true for religion in slightly different ways. Religion can meet the need for Safety & Security when looking to a Higher Power for protection and a promise of life everlasting. It can provide Connection through the relationships that develop between like-minded individuals and the Connection with one's Higher Power. It can satisfy Significance as people rise in the ranks of their religion and are recognized for their adherence to the doctrine, volunteerism, and leadership. It can meet the Freedom need because within the dictates of most religions is free will, allowing many followers to feel free within their faith. It can satisfy Joy through peak experiences with a deity, the social events that are organized with members, and the good feelings one may gain by passing on "the good word."

Not only can something meet different needs for different people, but it can also meet multiple needs for one person. For example, my work satisfies my needs in a myriad of ways. Getting paid for my work meets my need for Safety & Security. It satisfies Connection because I often meet wonderful people who later become friends and colleagues. Being able to help people make better choices and achieve Mental Freedom meets my need for Significance, as I'm able to do something I'm good at while helping people improve their lives. It satisfies my need for Freedom because not only do I get to do things the way I want as my own boss, but I also get to travel all over the world. And finally, watching someone transform throughout the Mental Freedom Experience meets my need for Joy—the pinnacle of my work.

I have always found the concept of these basic human needs so fascinating and multi-faceted. It can be overwhelming when first diving in, but with time and practice, you can become quite adept at understanding what is motivating you at any given point in time.

Although these five basic needs are genetically programmed in everyone, we are not all born with equal abilities to satisfy them. Privilege, geography, knowledge, beliefs, and values are some factors that affect need-satisfaction. A tenant of Mental Freedom is that people are not born evil. We each have an innate conscience that helps us understand what's right and wrong, which is further shaped by our culture and the people in our lives—family, educators, mentors, and friends—we look to for direction. When your environment offers responsible ways to meet your needs, you will typically choose those paths. However, if those responsible paths are blocked off, you may take a path that hurts other people or breaks the law. Needs don't care how they are satisfied—only that they are, indeed, satisfied.

People are instilled with a motivation to meet their needs, but that motivation doesn't come with an instruction manual. We cannot choose to wait for the ideal circumstances to present themselves. If your ideal path is blocked, you will accept the path available to you. This explains why someone with a high need for

Significance can become the CEO of a Fortune 500 company, the leader of a social movement, or the leader of a gang. The same need is being satisfied despite the difference of those roles, and although motivation can be temporarily deterred by morals, it won't last forever.

Practice looking beyond your behavior to find the goal you're trying to accomplish with it. Sometimes you might use Connection behavior to gain more Significance, or Joy behavior to gain more Connection. For example, I know that experiencing joy while learning is desirable, so I create opportunities for fun in my Choice Theory workshops. This isn't so I can personally experience joy—Joy is a low need of mine. I create Joy-focused experiences to gain Connection with participants and Significance as an instructor. What you're trying to achieve is more indicative of the need that is driving the behavior. You can identify the need that is motivating you from the inside by asking, "What is it that I want to accomplish with this behavior? Is it Safety & Security, Connection, Significance, Freedom, Joy, or some combination?"

Let us begin by looking at the genetically programmed needs as if there are no contextual pressures. In the section that follows, I will describe traits, qualities, characteristics, behaviors, likes, and dislikes for each of the five needs. It is extremely unlikely one of the following descriptions will perfectly describe you, as your dominant need is moderated by your other needs. The five needs are multi-dimensional, not one-dimensional, and their satisfaction levels are in constant flux. As you get to know the needs individually and understand how they manifest, the goal isn't to identify which of the five needs define you: "I'm a Connection person!" No single need offers such a neat fit, as all five exist in each of us. However, you can determine your need-strength profile—the size of your buckets—by using this information to identify patterns throughout your lifetime. From there, you can begin to uncover each of their satisfaction levels.

If one description fits you more than any other, it is likely your dominant need-strength. Typically, we work at filling our biggest buckets every day but can neglect the smaller ones for a short time.

Connection

When pressed on which need was most important, Dr. Glasser resolved it was the need for Connection because it's through our connections with people that we get all our other needs met. Even if it isn't your strongest need, it's still the most significant. Humans are hardwired to need relationships and places where they feel they belong. This is true for everyone, but there are those who need it more than others.

Centered around relationships, harmony, and quality time, the Connection need is replenished not only with intimacy and romance but also with time shared with family, friends, and pets. People who are most often motivated by Connection like to spend time with others, avoid conflict whenever possible, and help those in need. They enjoy socializing and generally have a high degree of empathy, allowing them to accurately assess the energy of those around them. Strong Connection people find it easy to be open with others and appreciate others being open with them, and they are welcoming to new people. They like being involved in their communities, participating in groups, and collaborating with others. Connection-dominant people are more likely to be people-pleasers, as harmonious relationships are their comfort zone.

Connection encompasses the values of harmony, kindness, charity, accommodation, cooperation, and collaboration.

People most motivated by Connection tend to avoid superficial interactions and relationships, but when it comes to people they care about, they will avoid setting boundaries and creating conflict, even when it could be the best thing for their Mental Freedom.

Strong Connection people have the superpowers of relationship-building, getting along well with others, accurately reading people's moods, mediating conflict between others, and creating an extensive support system for themselves. Weaknesses include expecting more from others than they are willing to give, unintentionally violating people's privacy, and being prone to loneliness.

You might see a lot of yourself in this description, but no one is exclusively motivated by Connection. For example, if you're feeling held back by the energy you spend servicing your loved ones, Significance will step in to motivate you to gain the confidence to follow your passion. Freedom and Joy might scream at you to draw boundaries and make time for yourself. Safety & Security can prevent you from making a decision against your best wishes to benefit someone else.

Safety & Security

Just from the name, some would think Safety & Security is the most important need. After all, how can you meet your other needs without feeling safe and secure? But there are many people who choose to put Safety & Security aside because other needs take precedence—take firefighters, police, or extreme sports athletes, for example. Then there are people with addictions, suicidal ideation, or eating disorders. Sometimes, people with terminal illnesses refuse life-prolonging treatment to satisfy needs that are stronger for them than Safety & Security.

The need for Survival, as Dr. Glasser calls it, is mostly physiological, involving such things as food, air, shelter, exercise, good health, and reproductive sex (for the survival of the species). However, it also encompasses the need to feel safe and secure, which is more psychological than physiological.

The need for Safety & Security can motivate behaviors like saving money, planning for the future, and maintaining healthy habits. Prioritizing safety over most everything, Safety & Security-dominant people proceed with caution and avoid risks. They plan for the long haul and generally find it difficult to embrace spontaneity. If diagnosed with a terminal illness, they will pursue extraordinary measures to prolong their lives.

Safety & Security highlights the values of responsibility, safety, organization, and preparedness.

The superpowers of Safety & Security are planning and protection. People motivated most by this need are usually experts at uncovering the dangers in everything. If the danger is too great, they will go into protection mode or find a way to mitigate the danger with proper planning. On the other hand, strong Safety & Security people have a propensity to guilt others into conforming to what will be most comfortable for them, which can look like pressuring their loved ones to not take the risks they feel called to take. This overprotective tendency can stunt not only the growth of those around them but also themselves; opportunities are missed when fear and anxiety prevent them from leaving their comfort zones.

The other needs will mitigate behavior motivated solely by Safety & Security. Imagine you're feeling extremely bored and are tired of playing it safe, Joy might motivate you to take risks and seek adventure. Freedom and Significance can push you to make a scary, life-changing decision with a potentially major payoff.

Significance

Significance equates to Glasser's need for Power, which has three ways of being satisfied: to power *over* others, to power *with* others, and to develop power *within*. To power over others is to use controlling behaviors like bullying, intimidation, and manipulation, which prevent those being controlled from meeting their own needs. Sometimes, in crisis situations, it is preferable for a leader to take control and power over others to get them to safety. To power with others involves working with others toward common goals, though this requires cooperation throughout the team. People who have power within have accomplished things that are important to them; they have found what they are good at and pursue it proudly. Cultivating power within is the most responsible and efficient way to satisfy Significance, as it does not interfere with others meeting their needs and cultivating power for themselves.

Significance motivates the desire to accomplish goals, make an impact, master new skills, be in the spotlight, and leave a legacy. Ambitious and decisive, Significance-dominant people are natural leaders who strive to be respected. They have a positive image of themselves, seek to gain status and positions of importance, and are naturally competitive. People motivated by Significance often stand up for their beliefs and can easily persuade others to adopt their way of thinking. Significance leads people away from situations where they might be disrespected, overlooked, or discounted. Strong Significance people will avoid situations where they aren't in charge or control, they try to avoid apologizing and admitting they were wrong. Being in control is their comfort zone.

The values motivated by Significance are respect, hard work, competition, recognition, success, accomplishment, and high self-worth.

The superpowers of Significance are accomplishing goals, decisiveness, and leading others. Strong Significance people are the embodiment of the Hunter S. Thompson quote, "Anything worth doing is worth doing well." Weaknesses include being overbearing, critical, and impatient with others as they meander toward their goals rather than tackle them. (Setting goals and crushing them is called a Significance superpower for a reason; not everyone has it.) Significance-dominant people are often perfectionists and workaholics, and when there are no opportunities to excel, they might misbehave.

Maybe you just learned you're a Significance-dominant person, but the other needs will direct your energy elsewhere. For example, you're feeling like you take life too seriously and are burnt out by always striving to do your best, Freedom might suggest breaking the rules, Joy might suggest taking a vacation, and Connection might cry out for a community of people who will nourish you.

Freedom

The need for Freedom encompasses physical and emotional freedom, and there are two types: There is freedom *from* (weight, restriction, and control, for example) and there is freedom *to* (have the things you want, do the things you want, and be the person you want to be).

Strong Freedom people feel driven to do what they want, when they want, without restrictions. Fiercely independent, they question the status quo and challenge authority. They might feel inclined to make a choice against their best interest just to do the opposite of what someone told them to do. They dislike having limited options, preferring to think outside the box, explore alternatives, and do things their own way; they deeply value the ability to engage their creativity. Freedom-dominant people tend to love traveling, overseeing their own schedule, and spending time alone. Living with an open mind, they are accepting of themselves and others. Spontaneity is their comfort zone, as they usually opt for adventure over the mundane.

Freedom-dominant people value alone time, creativity, privacy, adventure, spontaneity, and personal choice over obligation.

The superpowers of Freedom are creativity, open-mindedness, adaptability, and speaking truth to power. Weaknesses include avoiding asking people for help, even if it's desperately needed. They can lash out when feeling boxed in—stuck among people who feel controlling and in situations that lack options. Going through life considering only what is best for them, they sometimes lack regard for how their decisions affect others, resulting in selfish or destructive behavior.

Elements of all the other needs will manage the strong pull of Freedom. Let's say you have been spending a lot of time alone; you just returned from a month-long camping trip. With your Freedom bucket overflowing, neglected Connection will call you to see your loved ones. Joy, along with Safety & Security, might nudge you toward returning to your daily routine and making time for relaxation and your hobbies.

Joy

People with a high need for Joy are motivated to seek it in one or more of the following ways: play, humor, relaxation, or learning. People can enjoy all forms equally, or they may relax more than they learn or learn more than they play.

Do you tend to avoid things you perceive as being absent of joy? Do you have a great sense of humor and like to laugh? Is making others laugh a priority for you? Do you seek learning opportunities for the joy of discovery? Do you prioritize relaxation? Then you might have a high need for Joy.

People strongly driven by Joy gravitate toward adventure, relaxation, or discovering new things. Depending on the type of Joy they pursue, they can be described as funny, creative, adventurers, lifetime learners, practical jokers, experimenters, or experts in self-care. They have unlimited interests and relish hobbies, from the wild and kinetic to the quiet and meditative. They strive to keep the mood light and love to laugh, especially at themselves. They dislike seriousness and boredom. Professionals of sarcasm, they don't shy away from having fun at other people's expense, and often, that's how they show their love. Happiness is their comfort zone.

The strong values of Joy are recreation, free time, learning, humor, and relaxation.

The superpowers of Joy are having a great sense of humor, putting a smile on everyone's face, being present in the moment, and lightening the mood, particularly in tense situations. Weaknesses include boredom, going too far with humor and offending others, and lacking empathy—for example, trying to turn sober occasions into something fun.

The other needs will round out the edges of being exclusively motivated by Joy. For example, you're feeling exhausted from constantly being the life of the party and spending energy cheering people up. Safety & Security and Freedom might push you to withdraw and rejuvenate yourself. Significance may demand you make time to nourish it away from all the fun.

Need-Strength Bias

This chapter was written to help you recognize the needs that shape your personality and motivate your decisions so you can better understand yourself. However, as you were reading, it's likely you were considering which needs might be driving other people in your life. Remember that it is extremely difficult to judge what needs are motivating another person just by seeing the behaviors they engage in. You cannot know what the motivation is for those behaviors unless you ask—and even then, this person must understand how the five needs operate within themselves before they can communicate an accurate answer.

When a couple is in conflict, one thing I've seen in my many years of working with couples is that they will often assign Significance as the motivation behind their partner's behavior; they are experiencing frustration and assume it's because their partner is trying to control them. Without saying they are wrong, I'll ask, "If Significance weren't an option, what other need could be motivating their behavior?" This is meant to shift the person from blaming to understanding.

People generally gravitate toward those they have things in common with, such as occupations, social interests, hobbies, and so on. This indirectly results in gravitating toward those who are motivated by similar need-strengths, as people can become confused or annoyed with those who are motivated by different needs. People have an inherent bias to be judgmental and mistrustful toward differences, but this typically comes from a place of limited understanding. For example, as a Connection person, it's difficult for me to understand people who prefer to be alone; I can't think of a situation where I would prefer solitude over time with someone I enjoy. As a strong Freedom person, it is challenging to understand why someone wouldn't stand up for things that matter. I am strongly against injustice and speak out every chance I get, I have been labeled a rebel at work, and I will never understand the phrase, "Go along to get along." Armed with this knowledge, I am working on understanding these differences in others without bias—but it is difficult!

What follows is not meant to be stereotypes based on different need-strengths. Rather, it describes a general pattern of behavior many of us follow. There will always be exceptions, including extraordinary people who learned to overcome bias or seem to have never had it.

Connection-dominant people tend to judge people mostly driven by Significance and Freedom, the two biggest challengers of Connection. Describing a person high in Significance, Connection-dominant people might fail to mention how driven, goal-oriented, and focused a Significance-driven person can be—instead focusing on the Significance-dominant person's need to control things, forge ahead without input, and always have the last word. Describing Freedom-driven people, Connection people tend to focus on their selfishness, irresponsibility, and isolationist habits rather than seeing them as flexible, creative, and challengers of the status quo.

People mostly motivated by Freedom will likely share the same challenges with Significance-driven people mentioned above, in addition to Connection and Safety & Security. Through the Freedom lens, the Connection-driven desire to support and encourage people, to sense distress in others, or to help others feel welcome will be ignored. It's more likely that Freedom-dominant people will notice their violations of privacy, constant chatter, and people-pleasing tendencies. Safety & Security-driven people will seem inflexible, scared of everything, and cheap rather than prepared, future-oriented, and protective of those they care about.

Safety & Security-driven people will struggle with people motivated by Freedom and Joy. Freedom people appear selfish, irresponsible, and distant. Describing Joy-driven people, Safety & Security-dominant people may call them lazy (the relaxation type), flippant (the sense of humor type), silly (the play type) or pedantic (the learning type). It's unlikely Safety & Security people would describe them as present, knowledge-seeking, adventurous, or fun-loving.

Those with a strong Significance motivator might struggle with those who are driven by Connection, as they are more focused on people than getting things done; Freedom, because they are too absent and self-centered; and Joy, because they goof around and avoid hard work.

Joy-driven people will tend to struggle with those motivated by Significance and Safety & Security, viewing the Significance-driven person as controlling and authoritarian and the Safety & Security person as the proverbial stick in the mud.

After disclosing in a presentation that I am a Connection-driven person, a Significance-driven person asked me if all I wanted was for other people to like me since I'm so driven by Connection. I remember initially feeling insulted; I felt completely misunderstood. Then I remembered, I was being misunderstood. It is difficult for a Significance-driven person to see a Connection-driven person in a positive light.

Remember these key points about needs:

1. Our need-strength profile affects how we view the world.
2. All needs have positive and negative qualities associated with them, and whichever you experience depends on your perception.
3. We can be biased against people with need-strengths that challenge our own.
4. We can overcome our bias through motivation, commitment, and a genuine effort to understand and appreciate those who are different.

Keep in mind the information in this section was presented as if one need has exclusive control, which is not realistic. These stereotypical descriptions were designed to reveal patterns in your own life, and now, you can move forward through this book having gained insight into how your unique need-strength profile influences your behavior and relationships.

Use self-evaluation to ascertain your bias level; put in the effort to *really* listen to those you don't understand to uncover the positive side of their qualities. When you think something judgmental toward someone, ask yourself, "Is it possible for me to view this scenario through a positive lens?" I try to live by these words: If I don't like you very much, I just need to get to know you better. But as a Connection-driven person, wanting to get to know people is inherently easy for me and something I'm motivated to do, and that isn't true for everyone. Understanding how your need-strength profile determines what is inherently easy or difficult for you is an invaluable tool throughout your journey to Mental Freedom.

Experiencing conflict with a person because you're focused on the things that frustrate you while ignoring the things you could learn to appreciate will affect the amount of Mental Freedom you experience.

Advanced Mental Freedom

Every moment, as you experience life, you collect memories of things that met your needs in the past, and you spend some of your time imagining what could satisfy your needs in the future. But what if you come from an environment without many need-satisfying opportunities?

This is an advanced Mental Freedom concept—something you can work toward and access once you have done the work of this chapter. You can meet these needs by remembering and recognizing that you're made up of them. They aren't things you need to go out and get externally; they comprise your essential being.

For example, when you are looking outward for Safety & Security, be still, access your heart intelligence, and remember that you *are* safe. If you are seeking Connection outside yourself, recognize that you *are* love. When you are feeling insignificant or out of control, remember that you *are* significant. When you lack Freedom externally, remind yourself that you *are* free. And finally, when you aren't experiencing joy externally, recognize that you *are* joy.

Make your new daily mantra: "I am love, I am safe, I am significant, I am free, and I am joy." Of course, you can still access those things externally, but if you are struggling to do that, remember that you have an endless supply within yourself—you are made of safety, love, significance, freedom, and joy.

Summary:

1. Who you are as a person and what motivates you to behave in the way you do is largely determined by your five basic human needs: Safety & Security, Connection, Significance, Freedom, and Joy.

2. There are two factors that influence how strongly you feel the pull to satisfy one or more of these basic needs: the genetic strength of each need and how successful you are at satisfying them.

3. From the descriptions of the needs, try to recognize patterns present throughout your life to determine which needs motivate you the most.

4. Be aware of your biases and engage curiosity, understanding, and appreciation instead of judgment.

5. When you are ready to try some advanced Mental Freedom, it helps to remember that these are not external things you must acquire. By having internal ways to meet your needs, you have greater Mental Freedom. Remember that you are composed of these things, so they are always with you.

6. Use the mantra, "I am safe, I am love, I am significant, I am free, and I am joy."

Open Your Heart

Responsibility vs. Response-ability

"Look at the word responsibility—'response-ability'—the ability to choose your response. Highly proactive people recognize that responsibility. They do not blame circumstances, conditions, or conditioning for their behavior. Their behavior is a product of their own conscious choice, based on values, rather than a product of their conditions, based on feeling." –Stephen Covey

For the purposes of Mental Freedom, you are responsible for many things. You are responsible for the choices you make, and you are response-able, as Covey's quote above explains. There will be times when you respond from your moral, ethical, legal or emotional accountability. When you choose to be response-able, it should align with the person you want to be. If you aren't, then you sacrifice some of your Mental Freedom.

I first heard of this concept of responsibility versus response-ability from Stephen Covey in his book, *7 Habits of Highly Effective People*, and revisited it while talking with my then 36-year-old son, Dave. It was 2020, and we were talking about the Black Lives Matter movement, which I fully support. Dave was struggling with the concept. He believes he doesn't see color but sees people as people and does not consider himself a racist. He was struggling to accept that systemic racism is woven into the fabric of the country, still negatively impacting diverse groups in education, employment, accumulated wealth, finances, homeownership, healthcare and the criminal justice system, to name a few.

When I asked him why that concept was so challenging for

him, he responded by asking me who started systemic racism. I replied with, "The original slave owners." He persisted with, "But who were they, Mom?" I realized he wanted me to say, "White men," so I did. He said, "Right, and what am I? A white man. If I admit systemic racism exists, then, as a white male, I am responsible for it. That would make me racist, and I don't think I am." In that moment, it hit me that Dave, and many other white men, were confusing the difference between responsibility and response-ability.

Dave wasn't responsible for systemic racism or the 400 years of slavery in the U.S. that ended more than a century before he was born. He wasn't there when it began; he doesn't support it now. Clearly, he is not responsible for it, as he didn't directly participate in it. However, he has benefited from its legacy and can choose to be response-able. This means he has the ability to respond and make an impact.

After our discussion, he realized he could demonstrate his response-ability by taking steps to call for the dismantling of systemic racism. He can march in support of the Black Lives Matter movement and intentionally support Black-owned businesses. He can speak out to challenge inequities whenever he encounters them. He can vote for government officials who are supportive of the cause and advocate for reparations. Because there are things he can do right now, he is response-able.

Being response-able is not an obligation but it is almost always an option. If you have the ability to respond and decide to do nothing, you become responsible for doing nothing. Remember the quote by Edmund Burke: "All it takes for the perpetuation of evil is for good men to do nothing."

Please note, I am not saying white people don't have a moral obligation to dismantle systems of racial inequality. There are also individuals who are responsible for perpetrating acts of discrimination against people from various racial, ethnic, religious, and sexual backgrounds. For the purposes of Mental Freedom, they are responsible because they are actively participating. Others are response-able if they choose to be.

We sacrifice our Mental Freedom when we shirk our responsibility, judge ourselves culpable for things that we aren't culpable for, use our influence to try and control others into doing things our way, and take responsibility for things we didn't do.

Distinguishing the differences between what you are responsible for, what you bear culpability for, what you aren't responsible for and the many ways you can demonstrate your response-ability is how I like to begin the journey to Mental Freedom.

Responsibility

Shirking Responsibility

Refusing to take responsibility for your actions and thoughts will always stand in the way of achieving Mental Freedom.

One of the reasons people avoid taking responsibility is fear of punishment, as our actions can lead to unpleasant and sometimes painful consequences. When you own what you're responsible for, you can face external consequences for what you did. Even worse than the external consequences imposed by others, however, is the punishment you perpetrate on yourself.

Taking responsibility does not mean you have to beat yourself up. One of Mental Freedom's premises is that everyone is doing the best they can at any moment to get what they want. Making mistakes can teach you better ways to get what you want, and they can force you to look at things in a new way; suddenly, you realize your priorities were mixed up and you want something else instead. Whatever you would do differently *now*, with this new knowledge, was not available to you at *that* moment—so please, forgive yourself. You may have done something you now regret, but understand that you did the best you knew, at that time, to get what you wanted. Accept your perfectly imperfect self and make today a new day. This is why accepting responsibility is an act of self-love.

Taking Responsibility

You are 100% responsible for everything you do, including those things you are capable of doing but choose not to. If you witness a crime and you turn around and go the other way, you are responsible for that decision. I'm not saying the decision is right or wrong. You might have endangered yourself by offering help. However, you had a decision to make, and you chose to walk away, and you're responsible for that choice—just as you would have been responsible for intervening. Everything you do is a choice (hence the name of my podcast, *Life = Choices; Choices = Life*, LifeEqualsChoices.com). If someone threatens your life, you would likely choose to comply because the consequences of non-compliance would be too great. While you wouldn't be culpable, you are still responsible for what you did simply because you did it.

In Mental Freedom, there are five things you are responsible for: 1) your actions and thoughts; 2) satisfying your needs; 3) your own happiness; 4) the solutions to your problems and 5) your half, and only your half, of all your relationships.

Your Actions and Thoughts

Everything you do is a choice, even when it doesn't feel like it. Sometimes we have choices but perceive them as bad, and while that may be true, it doesn't negate the fact that there are choices. Even if threatened with the loss of your life, you can decide there are things worth dying for. It might be the last thing you want to happen, but you are responsible for all you do and the resulting consequences, whether intended or not, without exception.

On the other hand, you are also responsible for your strengths and accomplishments. It is not your responsibility to dim your light so others can feel better about themselves. However, if you are uncomfortable in the spotlight, own your successes privately if you prefer, but whatever you do, don't attribute your successes to luck. Luck has nothing to do with it. If you are a spiritual person, you may give glory to your Higher Power but feel gratified in knowing it was *you* your Higher Power was working through. You can always pay it forward or engage in a random act of kindness you tell no one about. The warm, joyful energy of doing something kind and affecting positive change in the world will be your reward.

Unless you are very humble, introverted or shy, it's relatively easy to take responsibility for our successes. People like to be responsible for the good things they do, as these things often become a source of pride. It becomes increasingly more difficult, however, when things don't turn out as you planned.

Nobody likes to be blamed for things; that never feels good. If you make a decision that doesn't work out as expected, finding someone else to blame will detract from your Mental Freedom.

Making mistakes doesn't make you a bad person. Once you claim responsibility, you can fix it or make restitution, and you can begin to create opportunities to grow from your mistakes. The great thing about mistakes is there is always something to learn from them, but you'll likely miss the lesson if you expend your energy trying to find a rationale for why you aren't responsible.

As if being responsible for your behavior isn't enough, you are also responsible for your thoughts—maybe not 100% responsible for them, as there are those intrusive thoughts we don't consciously invite into our heads. However, we are responsible for the overall tone of our thoughts because we have the ability to control this by thinking of something more preferable. In order to achieve Mental Freedom, you'll want to also take responsibility for your feelings by choosing the thoughts that lead you to act in alignment with the person you most want to be.

Satisfying Your Own Needs

As mentioned in the previous chapter, everyone has five basic needs that motivate all behavior. We experience these needs in varying degrees of strength. Each need is a different size cup, a unique set for each person, and ideally, all the cups are perfectly filled. Even when your weakest need, your smallest cup, is being neglected, it will be empty and its need for satisfaction will become impossible to ignore. When you experience depletion in one or more of your needs, it's easy to look outside yourself to fulfill them. This typically results in holding other people accountable for meeting your needs for you. Satisfying *your* needs is never someone else's responsibility. While you will have people in your life who make it easier to meet your needs through your relationships with them, it is never *their* responsibility. It is always your responsibility to meet your needs in a responsible way.

Meeting your needs in a responsible way means getting what you need without preventing others from getting what they need. If you see yourself as a loyal, devoted partner who is not getting the connection from your partner you need, being responsible means finding other ways to achieve more connection in your life without dishonoring your relationship with your partner.

Yes, you have the right to ask for what you want in any relationship but know it is never the other person's responsibility to provide it for you. If they give you what you ask for, great. If they don't, then taking responsibility would require you to seek new ways to satisfy your needs.

Your Own Happiness

When your needs are met, you tend to feel happy and content. Whenever you tell yourself you'll be happy when (fill in the blank), you relinquish responsibility for your own happiness. Happiness is a choice, therefore, you are responsible for deciding to be happy now. You can be happy for no particular reason, as Marci Shimoff writes in her bestselling book, *Happy for No Reason*. Yes, you are responsible for meeting your needs and your own happiness, but you are not responsible for meeting someone else's needs or making them happy. If you have been doing that, please stop; it's an exercise in futility. The best thing you can give your partner, parent, child, boss, coworker, or friend is a version of yourself who is contented.

If you tie your happiness to something someone else *must* do, it can feel like a leash that constantly keeps happiness out of your reach. Take responsibility by understanding that happiness comes from the inside, not the outside.

When you operate with an internal control mindset, you realize you can be content, and even happy, despite your outside circumstances. Make it a practice to inventory all the positive things in your life. Give gratitude for all you have. Learn to enjoy the journey, no matter what else is happening around you.

The Solutions to Your Problems

You are responsible for the solutions to your own problems, and yet, we often expect other people to fix them for us. When working with couples to research my book, *Secrets of Happy Couples*, I identified two common complaints: piles of dirty clothes, and letting the car run low on fuel. However, whether the person felt frustrated that their partner's dirty clothes didn't make it to the hamper, or to see that fuel light in the dashboard, it was the person complaining who had the problem, not the perpetrator. The person who is most upset about a situation owns the problem; the other person is merely doing what makes sense and works for them. It's not personal, as you will learn in chapter four, "The Unconditional Trust Challenge."

By the way, if you are upset about your partner not putting their clothes in the hamper, I recommend doing it yourself. Or, if you're upset at your partner's nearly empty fuel tank, fill it for them. The only thing that prevents you from doing this is believing that your partner is supposed to rectify *your* problems.

Your Half of Your Relationships

Finally, you are responsible for your half of all your relationships. When you are in a relationship with someone, you are each responsible for meeting your own needs and achieving your corresponding happiness. You are responsible for everything you do in that relationship, including the thoughts you maintain about your relationship and the other person. Neither of you is responsible for fixing the other person by critiquing or controlling, and there is a shared responsibility for the success of the relationship.

You are responsible for doing your best, without compromising your own needs or contentment, to avoid making it difficult for the other person to satisfy their needs. If you fail to do that, you prioritize your own needs with no responsibility to your relationship, and that does not bode well for your relationship or your future happiness in it.

Culpability

One rainy day, I was walking on a crowded street in Hong Kong using an umbrella like everyone else, and occasionally, I would bump into someone else's umbrella. Was I responsible? Yes. Was I culpable, no. Of course, I would have been culpable if I did it to annoy someone who bumped into me.

You are culpable if you've done something wrong and are at fault for the consequences of your actions, particularly if you intended to do harm. Even if it wasn't intended, you are culpable if your reckless or negligent actions cause negative consequences. Although these experiences may represent the biggest challenge in accepting responsibility, Mental Freedom requires you to do so, *especially* when it's hard.

I worked with a client once whose husband drank a lot and did most of his drinking in secret. Most people didn't even know how much alcohol he consumed on any given day, and it was excessive. My client shared that one day, when she went to the water park with her husband and their children, he took their three-year-old son out into the water, and a wave knocked him right out of his grasp. Unbeknownst to her, he had been drinking. She watched for several heartbreaking seconds as her husband flailed around, trying to locate their son in the water. He finally did and carried him up on the beach unharmed. Of course, he wasn't intending to drown their child, but due to his recklessness, the child was put in danger nonetheless. This makes him both responsible *and* culpable.

On the other hand, you can render yourself culpable for something that *wasn't* your fault. For example, when parents divorce, children often believe it is their fault. I have even heard stories of children who say out loud to their parent, "I wish you were dead," and said death occurs, resulting in that child developing the magical thinking that they are culpable for their parent's death.

I knew a man who was home overnight with his two children since his wife was out of town. His daughter needed a ride to school in the early morning hours for a class trip. Not wanting to wake his 10-year-old son, he left him sleeping while he drove his daughter the eight miles to her school. When he returned home, the house was engulfed in flames, and his precious son died. He was responsible for leaving his child home because he did that, but he was not culpable. Taking on that culpability tortured this father. It took him several years before he could reengage with life. During that time, he was judge, jury, and executioner, sentencing himself to the mental prison he had constructed for his punishment.

Before holding yourself culpable for things you are merely responsible for, ask yourself if you intended that outcome or if you were negligent, allowing that outcome to occur. The next chapter will address overcoming the issue of judging yourself as culpable when you are not, as you will learn to develop some compassion and forgiveness for yourself. Conversely, you will also learn how to let go of holding someone else culpable for something that was truly unintended.

Levels of Accountability

There are three basic levels of accountability to analyze: situations where you are 100% in control, situations where you have influence or are being influenced, and situations where you have zero control or influence. Let's dive into the differences and what to do about each of them.

Total Control

In situations where you have total control, it's easy to see your responsibility. If *you* did it, you are responsible. When my children were about eight and ten, we drove to a pond that was on our property, and our dog and her puppies followed us. We had a nice time swimming, and when it was time to return to the house, we all piled into the car. I started it, looked behind me, and proceeded to back up over something I hadn't seen in the tall grass. I got out of the car and saw it was one of those puppies. I didn't mean to do it; it was an accident. But nevertheless, I did it. It was hard to admit to my kids that I killed one of those puppies, but I was responsible for it. We call these occurrences accidents, but we still bear responsibility; however, I bore no culpability in that incident. I was in a field where the grass hadn't been mowed, and the puppy was not visible in my mirrors. I evaluated what happened and realized I wasn't being reckless, nor did I intend to do it.

When you take responsibility for the things you have done, you can fix them or make restitution. Alternatively, if you've determined they cannot be fixed, you can release the hopelessness that comes from being unable to affect a positive change and instead focus on what you've learned and will do differently in the future.

Influence

There are situations when you may have influence. Influence is never guaranteed, but if you are experiencing something you don't like and you think you have the power to change the outcome, you are one hundred percent responsible for how you use your influence. There's a distinction between informational and controlling influence: We generally relish informational influence while resisting controlling influence, and we must also consider times when someone else is attempting to influence us.

If you have information that can help a situation's outcome improve, you are responsible for whether you share that information and the way in which you share it. The responsibility for the outcome rests with them. You are fully responsible for sharing the information while the other person is fully responsible for their decisions and behaviors resulting from learning the information.

I know this feels like common sense, but it isn't so easy to put into practice. For every individual who has tried to influence the wardrobe of their partner and failed, understand that what they finally choose to wear is not your responsibility. Will you be judged because of it by people who want to hold you responsible? Perhaps—and how you manage that judgment becomes something you are responsible for.

The way in which you share information is critical. With informational influence, you share information simply for the other person to make a more informed decision. It is not your responsibility to get people to do things the way you want them done, as if your way is the best or only way. When you use controlling influence, however, you share information as a way of coercing someone into doing what *you* think is best, attempting to control them. This is not conducive to creating the closeness you crave in your important relationships. No one likes to be controlled.

Sometimes we are the people wielding the influence, and other times, someone wields their influence on us; the amount of influence they have is directly proportional to the closeness of the relationship you share as measured by trust and respect.

The question is, can you look at yourself in the mirror and feel good about how you used your influence?

Informational influence

Informational influence occurs when you share information with someone that may impact their decisions or behavior. You don't have a vested interest in the outcome, but you believe not sharing what you know could result in negative consequences. An example might be that you just pulled into port from a fishing expedition because a storm was coming in. You see another boat headed out to where you just came from and decide to give the information about the high swells to the other fishermen. Their decision to go or stay has no impact on you, but you chose to be response-able by using informational influence.

The goal isn't to change someone's mind about something,

although that may be the result of your influence. It's to provide additional information so others can make a more informed decision. Although it is never guaranteed, we generally have informational influence with people who like, trust, and respect us.

Another example is if someone mentions how they plan to get from point A to B and you happen to know there is traffic along that route: You can influence the person's decision by sharing that information. The second axiom of Choice Theory psychology is, "All we can give [to] or get from other people is information."

If someone you care about is contemplating an action that you think may have negative consequences, you could share information with them that may change their mind. Parents have influence over their children when they are small, and how they choose to exercise that influence will determine how those children respond later in life when their parents continue their attempts at influence.

Many years ago, my son asked his wife if she knew the difference between me and her mother. She said she didn't, and he responded, "Your mom tells us what to do; my mom makes suggestions." That was a proud-Mama moment for me. I truly wish to be the kind of person who shares information but leaves decisions up to the people whose responsibility it is to make them and live with the results of those decisions.

You may make the choice to stay out of other people's business by avoiding giving advice to someone else. This makes you responsible for valuing a person's independence and privacy more than wanting to share what you know. It isn't a right or wrong choice because you never know how a person will respond to your influence. A person may take your advice and things could work out great. Conversely, they could take your advice and create a disaster for themselves. Whether you intervene or not, you are responsible for that choice.

You are responsible for choosing to not provide information, but even when you choose to share, you are not responsible for the choice that person makes to take a different route or stay their course.

Because I'm able to influence people with my words, I employ informational influence by using my platform as an ally. I work to educate and provide information that some people may not have considered through my blog (OlverInternational.com/Blog) and my podcast (OlverInternational.com/Podcast), where I invite thought leaders to discuss various topics, including a month dedicated to Diversity, Equity, Inclusion, and Belonging. My goal is not to change people's minds; I simply share information with those who are open to receiving it. When people disagree with me and try to convince me of their point of view, I stop trying to influence—not because I'm no longer an ally, but because I understand cognitive dissonance: If I keep forcefully pushing against what others believe, instead of enticing their curiosity, it can cause them to double-down on their original opinions, thus creating the opposite of what I had hoped to accomplish. Knowing when to use your influence and when to back off is a skill that comes with practice.

Controlling Influence

Controlling influence happens when you use whatever is available to you to get someone to do what you'd prefer them to do.

I remember when my son, Dave, turned 16 and wanted to buy a car. I wanted him to be safe, so I used controlling influence by offering to pay for half the car if he chose a car with a solid metal frame. Dave chose a Mitsubishi Eclipse, so I did not contribute. I wasn't mad he chose that, and I wasn't trying to *make* him do things my way, but I was unsuccessfully using my influence to tip the odds in the direction of safety for him and less worry for me.

People can also use influence in an irresponsible way. Choice Theory discusses the idea of meeting your needs responsibly, which is meeting your needs without preventing others from meeting theirs. People who use influence to control others typically achieve compliance because they have made it too painful for the other person to continue otherwise. This can happen by force, psychological influence or emotional blackmail. A person who chooses to influence in this way either has negative intent, is attempting to force someone against their own best interests, or truly wants to help but doesn't have the right to intervene. They are attempting to force an outcome by using controlling influence. When you employ influence with power and control for your own purposes, you may get what you want temporarily, but you are simultaneously responsible and culpable for the outcomes, which usually include damage to relationships.

When You are Being Influenced

Being on the receiving end of someone attempting to influence you presents a series of choices. Whether or not the information is welcome, you get to decide if you will take it into consideration and allow it to influence your course—and you are responsible for these choices. Someone gave you information, and how you decide to let it influence you is your responsibility.

When you are on the receiving end of painful, irresponsible influence intended to control your behavior, you are responsible for how you prioritize and weigh the implied or explicit consequences of non-compliance. If the consequences are not too great, you might choose to disregard them and act in the way *you* prefer. If the consequences are more than you want to bear, you will likely choose to do what the controller wants. In that case, you are still responsible, but you're not culpable. The person exerting that control is the one culpable. However, even though you should not be blamed for actions you take under duress, you are still responsible for them.

No Control

This last category—the things you can't control—often produces consequences you don't like. Of course, there are plenty of positive things that happen that are out of your control—winning the lottery, being invited to a coveted social event, making a random connection that turns into a job opportunity—but they don't tend to reduce your Mental Freedom. The circumstances that cause pain and inconvenience are what's noticed most.

You can sacrifice your Mental Freedom by taking responsibility for random events, other people's actions, and even crimes committed against your person, like abuse and assault—none of which you can control. This contributes to the mental prison you can potentially create for yourself. Once you determine what you're responsible for and stop owning things beyond your control, you can free yourself from any self-created guilt or misery.

Another way you can blame yourself for things beyond your control is by saying things like, "I knew I shouldn't have installed a wood stove; that's what caused the fire," or "We shouldn't have moved into a house so close to the river; now many of our things are ruined by the flooding." Blaming yourself puts your brain to work finding a way it could've been controlled or prevented in the event something similar happens again. This is a fool's errand, though, because the situations are uncontrollable. Blaming yourself won't yield a different outcome next time, nor will it allow you to claim your Mental Freedom.

I worked many years with children in foster care, many of whom had suffered abuse and neglect at the hands of their parents for which they often took responsibility. This happens in adult abusive relationships, too. Without control, you bear no responsibility. A perpetrator will instill the belief that their victim is to blame as a control tactic. When victims are groomed to take responsibility for what their perpetrator did, it makes it easier for the perpetrator to continue their abuse.

Additionally, people tend to take responsibility for their own abuse because holding the perpetrator responsible, and even culpable, might be too painful. If this describes you, know that this is not the path to Mental Freedom. You need to reframe your thoughts to place the responsibility and culpability at the feet of the person who committed the offense—only then can you unlock the doors to the mental prison you have placed yourself in. Mental Freedom only comes when you take responsibility for what's yours and release what isn't.

It's been established that you are not responsible for what you can't control, but it's worth emphasizing that you are responsible for how you respond. You can resign to being a victim, you can recover so you can help others in similar circumstances, or you can land anywhere in between. Mental Freedom cannot be found in the role of the victim—you will need to exercise formidable control over your recovery, and this may require professional help. Asking for what you need is a sign of strength, not weakness.

Achieving Mental Freedom after experiencing trauma can seem impossible, but it just takes work and time. It will require you to recognize what happened to you was not your fault. Barring permanent physical injury, you can have a full recovery. The work to find yourself again after trauma is beyond the scope of this book, but if you're looking for resources, I recommend Melanie Smith's book, *Unfinished Business*, Gigi Kilroe's book, *From Within*, and Monika Korra's book, *Kill the Silence*.

If you take responsibility for something like a flood, fire, or tornado, you decide it must be payback for something you feel guilty about—as if some divine being was punishing you. You are not responsible for such tragic events, but you are responsible for how you respond and recover from them.

What is Not Your Responsibility

It is challenging to take responsibility where it's due while keeping boundaries around things that aren't your responsibility—like meeting other people's needs, creating their happiness, or finding the solutions to their problems.

Take being a parent, for example. It's hard to watch your children make choices that may have negative consequences for them. I wanted to save my sons from unpleasantness; I wanted to stop them from doing things I thought were mistakes. But then there were times I tried to make my kids take responsibility for my happiness. When my children were toddlers, before I learned Choice Theory, I let them know that their actions "made" me sad or frustrated so they would do something more in line with the things that would "make" me happy. Eventually, I learned that meeting my own needs is 100% my responsibility. While I can help create a relationship where my children and I can work together to meet our needs, I can't do that *for* them any more than they can do that for me.

A parent taking responsibility for their adult children's decisions is typically a result of feeling guilty for the choices the child makes—a common occurrence in instances of irresponsible behavior, like addiction, for example. A parent can feel compelled to take responsibility because they feel it must have been the personal decisions they made during their kid's childhood that led to their troubled adulthood. For example, a client of mine has a daughter in her thirties who is in an abusive relationship. The mother asked me, "What did I do wrong that would allow her to stay in such a relationship?" Yes, she is responsible for the decisions she made while parenting her child, but she is not responsible for her grown daughter's decisions. One cannot experience Mental Freedom when holding onto this kind of guilt and responsibility.

Parents typically do their best to pass on what they believe is right and wrong to help their kids make sense of the world, hopefully resulting in them making good decisions. However, children become teenagers who turn into young adults, and eventually, parents get to relinquish their responsibility for the actions of their grown, adult children.

Children often grow up sharing a lot of the values their parents instilled in them, but I have yet to meet anyone who claims they share the exact values of their parents. On the other hand, there are adults who pride themselves on living a life in opposition to their parents' values. Whatever the case, adults have the right and responsibility to make their own decisions, even if their parents strongly disapprove.

As a parent, it can be extremely painful to witness your child making decisions you believe are not good for them; you truly identify with their pain and desperately want to save them from themselves. However, attempts to "fix" your grown child often communicate the message that they are broken—something is wrong that needs fixing. Even though you are operating out of love, they will feel criticized. Sometimes, their best defense is to push you away or, at the very least, stop listening to you. Sometimes, they'll go right out to do the opposite of what you want for them. In fulfilling what you believe are your parental duties, you'll likely make the situation worse.

The best thing you can do for the people you deeply care about, and for your own Mental Freedom, is to hold them responsible for their own lives. People rarely learn lessons from other people's experiences; most of us had to touch the stove for ourselves even after being told it was painfully hot. Miraculously, once you stop trying to change or fix people in your life, they won't be actively pushing back against your wishes, leaving them space to potentially come around to your way of thinking. When you stop taking responsibility for things that aren't yours, you create a vacuum—and the Universe abhors a vacuum. The person whose responsibility it is will often step forward into their responsibility and heal themselves.

It's important to remember that everyone has their own path. Sometimes, people are here to provide examples for others— they are meant to go through something, heal, and help others in similar situations. On your own path, and for the sake of Mental Freedom, you need to allow others in your life to follow their own course without interference.

Taking responsibility for things other people do never leads to Mental Freedom—but what if your job involves being responsible for others? Counselors are responsible for their clients; teachers are responsible for their students; supervisors are responsible for their workers. Or are they?

With Mental Freedom, I've learned that I am responsible for being the best counselor I can be, but my clients are responsible for the choices they make. I am responsible for teaching my students the best way I can; they are responsible for their learning. I am responsible for leading my workers in the direction of my vision; they are responsible for how they choose to follow—or not.

To practice Mental Freedom, it is critical to understand what your responsibility is and what it is not. You are responsible for getting your own needs met and doing your best with your commitments. It is not your responsibility to get other people to do what you think is best. That is their responsibility.

This is easy to understand yet difficult to implement. Success comes with committed, dedicated practice.

Response-ability

In any situation, whether you're responsible or not, there is usually something you can do, making you response-able. You can choose to respond in a way that helps, has no effect, or makes it worse. You can also decide to not respond at all. Whatever your choice in the situation, you are 100% responsible for it.

Being response-able should not feel like a burden. It results from empathy—your innate desire to connect with others, sense their pain, and respond in a helpful way when you are able. Should you find yourself being response-able while feeling frustrated and resentful, consider pulling back a bit. If your response-ableness is a cultural norm, it helps to find a reason why you want to participate so you don't continue with resentment in your heart. This will be discussed in detail in chapter five, "Empowering vs. Victimizing Language."

When you choose response-ability, you take control of the only things you can control—your thoughts and actions. This has the potential to increase your Mental Freedom by enabling you to claim agency in situations where you might otherwise feel helpless. It's one of the reasons people bring homemade food to a place where someone might be sick or dying. There is nothing that can be done to stop the progression of the illness, but empathetic neighbors still try to lighten the load of those grieving.

How many times in our lives have we encountered someone we could have helped but didn't because it wasn't convenient? How many times have we kept silent when we had something important to say? How many times could we have bettered ourselves but didn't because we thought it might be too hard? Disregard those instances revealed by hindsight because you are not responsible for things you didn't know about. However, the deliberate decisions not to act—you are completely responsible for those.

Imagine you are walking in a big city and an unhoused person asks you for money for food. It is not your responsibility to give them money, but being response-able, you can give them some change, a significant sum, buy them food, or keep on walking by. Let's say you stop and give them $20, and unbeknownst to you, they use it to buy drugs. Are you responsible? Yes, just as they are responsible for their decision. Are you culpable? No—you believed they were going to buy food with it, and you didn't have time to go buy the food yourself. You chose to be response-able with an open heart, and while you're responsible for that decision, you are not culpable.

What about other people's feelings—are you responsible for those? No, you are not responsible for other people's perceptions and feelings. That responsibility belongs to the person who is perceiving and emoting. However, you can be response-able by considering your thoughts and actions and whether they contributed to the misunderstanding, frustration or pain of the other person, especially if this is someone you care about. Whenever there are unwanted consequences to your actions, even if you are not responsible for them, you can self-evaluate to determine what part, if any, might be your responsibility, and choose how you can be response-able. The goal is to balance your actions with your authentic self while being careful not to interfere with others.

You can't be response-able in the past, as that chapter of your life has already been written. Being response-able is a choice only available in the present, but you can't get a do-over on something you did or didn't do in the past. All that can be done in the present moment is to attempt to make the situation you find yourself in better, but there is no requirement to be response-able. It's your choice.

Before you decide whether you want to be response-able or walk away, ask yourself, "What kind of person do I want to be in this situation?" and then align your behavior with that version of yourself. Don't make your choices out of guilt or popular opinion. You are the person who must live with your decisions and behavior for the rest of your life, so choose what aligns with the best version of yourself.

Summary:

1. Mental Freedom comes when you take responsibility for what's yours:
    a. Everything you do, and think
    b. Satisfying your five basic needs
    c. Your own happiness
    d. The solutions to your problems
    e. Your half, and only your half, of all your relationships
    f. How you use your influence
    g. How you allow yourself to be influenced by others.
2. Mental Freedom increases when you stop taking responsibility for things you are not responsible for:
    a. The actions of others
    b. Random events
    c. Your trauma
    d. Your adult children
3. Deciding to be response-able can increase your Mental Freedom. While you may not own responsibility for a situation, there is usually something you can do to help if you choose to, and when you do, you are responsible for that decision and its consequences.

THE UNCONDITIONAL TRUST CHALLENGE

"When someone shows you who they are, believe them the first time. People know themselves much better than you do. That's why it's important to stop expecting them to be something other than who they are." –Maya Angelou

Trust is an interesting concept that is especially important for relationships, but typically, people only think about trusting someone to be the person they want them to be. It's wonderful when the people in our lives meet our expectations, but continuing to trust people will meet our expectations even when their actions indicate otherwise can sacrifice our Mental Freedom in a big way.

It's normal to maintain an idea in your head about how you want the important people in your life to act and carry expectations that they will do what they say they will.

People act in service of what they want, and the Unconditional Trust Challenge recognizes this. To participate in this challenge, you simply vow to trust everyone on the planet is doing their best to get what they want at that moment.

Taking on this challenge doesn't mean unconditionally trusting everyone will do what they say they'll do or that they'll do "the right thing," as defined by you. Some people think it's always right to tell the truth, and others can argue that being totally transparent can be unkind. Who is morally right? That determination would depend on what you value most—honesty and transparency or kindness.

Participating in the Unconditional Trust Challenge requires you to trust everyone for the one thing you are sure they will do: In every situation, people do their best with the information available to them to get what they want. Once you trust people this way, you can relinquish judgment about good, bad, right and wrong, and you will never be disappointed again. You accept everyone for doing their best to get what they want, and this acceptance sets you on the path to clarity, nonjudgment, compassion, and forgiveness.

Expectations

The Unconditional Trust Challenge begins with letting go of expectations. This is not an easy task, but it grants you the freedom to allow people to be who they are, which then leads to acceptance, and with acceptance comes serenity—just like the Serenity Prayer promises: *God grant me the serenity to accept the things I cannot change, courage to change the things I can and the wisdom to know the difference.*

If you stop having expectations of others, you will stop beating your head against that brick wall trying to change people into what you want them to be.

People give up their Mental Freedom when they become disappointed with people who don't match their expectations. Opportunities for disappointment can be found everywhere and, when encountered, people tend to tell themselves that life isn't fair and these things shouldn't happen, thereby placing themselves in the victim role—the furthest one can be from Mental Freedom.

The problem with having expectations of others is three-fold:

1. Your expectations are in your head, and typically, you don't communicate them or you don't communicate them well.
2. Your expectations are often based on perfection, and no one can measure up to that.
3. Your expectations are based on what *you* want, but people behave to get what *they* want. When you have a relationship with someone, whether romantic,

family, or friend, generally you want that person to be happy. Conversely, there will be things you want that have nothing to do with that other person that may lead to their disappointment, frustration, or anger.

If what the other person wants at a particular moment is for you to be happy, and they decide to be response-able, they will choose the best way they know to create happiness for you. However, no one can consistently prioritize another person's happiness over their own. Therefore, there will inevitably be times when the people you care about will make choices that don't align with what you'd prefer they do. When this happens, you might think, "I don't trust you anymore," unless you choose to implement the Unconditional Trust Challenge instead.

This quote by Kyle Cease dumbfounded me the first time I heard it: "No one's ever broken your heart; they've broken your expectations." Since I was the one who created my expectations, I was responsible for my own heartbreak—what an epiphany.

People in relationships tend to want a partner they can count on for certain things. They want to be able to trust their partner to maintain somewhat predictable behavior, but people don't always do that. Sometimes, people act in unprecedented ways, which leads to their partner believing their partner can't be trusted.

The Unconditional Trust Challenge involves recognizing that something might have occurred that shifted their priorities, and they responded by doing their best to get what they wanted, even if it was in a way that was outside their typical behavior. People also change; it could be that they are metamorphosing into a new version of themselves. For greater Mental Freedom, you want to be flexible enough that you can allow people you care about to engage in their own journeys of transformation.

When your goal is to understand the person's choices better, you might want to have a conversation about what changed. What did they want at that moment? Why did their priorities shift? Would they do it the same way next time?

It's perfectly all right to have expectations for yourself,

provided you aren't a perfectionist. If you are, your expectations are impossible to master, leaving you in a constant state of stress and frustration. For the sake of your Mental Freedom, be flexible with the expectations you have for yourself. If you're in a position where you rely on others, remember that you cannot control anyone other than yourself.

Adjusting the expectations you have for yourself and relinquishing the expectations you have for others result in great progress toward Mental Freedom. Here are some ways you can successfully accomplish this:

1. Avoid the comparison game. It's one you can't win. As Theodore Roosevelt said, "Comparison is the thief of joy." There will always be someone better at some things. If you must make comparisons, compare yourself to who you were yesterday, last week, or last year.

2. Instead of beating yourself up for what you haven't accomplished, give yourself credit for the things you have.

3. Invest time and energy in honing your passion every day so you can be better than you were yesterday.

4. Stop putting time, energy, and attention into things that aren't important to you. Everything can't be of equal value. Focus on what you have determined to be your most important priorities.

A Minor Choice Theory Tweak

I have been studying Choice Theory® psychology for more than 35 years. It includes the concept that people are doing their best in any given situation with the information available to them. I believed in that statement for much of those 35 years.

In Mental Freedom, I say it just a little bit differently and I believe it makes all the difference: *People are doing the best they can to get what they want with the information available to them at any given moment in time.*

There are two variables that can be adjusted when people are seeking different outcomes. They can change their focus to a different desire or they can develop new skills so they have better ways to get what they want.

The toddler who hits his brother over the head with a truck knows that hitting his brother is not a good thing to do, but at that moment, he wanted what his brother was playing with, and hitting him was the best way he knew to get it. The parent who abandons her child on a church step knows it may not be the best thing to do, but she wants her freedom more, and maybe she believes the child would be better off without her. The person who cheats on their spouse knows it may not be the best thing they can do at the time, but it's what they want at that moment. The non-monogamist may have been seeking attention, understanding, respect, variety, or avoidance of the bigger issues within their marriage.

Regardless of what you think about the rationality or morality of someone's motivation, everyone is always doing the best they can to get what they want at that moment.

We all have ideas about what we want the important people in our lives to act like. If every person in your life acted the way you wanted them to, your life would be substantially better, right? When they match what you want, you might recognize this as feeling trust in them. If they don't measure up to the idea you created in your head, you might recognize this as feeling unable to trust them.

The path to Mental Freedom is revealed when you stop trusting people to be who you want them to be and begin to trust them for who they have shown you they are until they consistently show you something different. Of course, people can change. If they consistently display different behavior, you can reevaluate your trust in them. But you can't force this change to happen. People change when they come to believe they will get more of what they want if they do things differently—not because they've noticed you want something different from them.

We can always trust *everyone* to do one thing in *every*

circumstance without exception, and maintaining *this* brand of trust will propel you on your journey to Mental Freedom. You can trust that every single person on the planet is going to do what they believe is their best option, in any situation, to get what they want based on the information available to them. If you care about them, isn't that what you want them to do? It's difficult to get angry at someone when you understand that they're doing the best they can to get what they want.

When someone inevitably does something that makes it difficult for you to get what you want, the Unconditional Trust Challenge asks you to not hold that person responsible for the frustration *you* have. In chapter seven, "Signals vs. Solutions," you will learn how to transform your frustration into something different and more positive.

Origin of the Unconditional Trust Challenge

In 2019, a major clash between my expectations and reality caused me to have a very painful three days. It's the last time I spent that long feeling sorry for myself because I've been using the Unconditional Trust Challenge ever since.

I had a good friend, Donny, with kidney disease, who had been on dialysis for several years and had begun to look extremely unhealthy. I kept our mutual friend who lives in California, Sam, informed of Donny's health. One day, I told Sam that he needed to come to Chicago because I wasn't sure how long Donny would be with us. Wanting to surprise Donny, he asked if I could pick him up at the airport and if he could stay at my place.

Of course, I agreed and had great plans for what our weekend together would entail. I picked him up from the airport, and we had a night of catching up on old times. The next day, I called Donny to ask if he could meet me for lunch and he agreed. Sam and I went to the restaurant early and when Donny arrived, he was pleasantly surprised to see Sam there. We had a great time eating, laughing, and reminiscing.

After a few hours, I went back to my place to let them have some time alone and casually asked them to let me know what was happening later. I foolishly sat by the phone waiting to hear from them, but I didn't hear from them until the next day. Sam and Donny came by to get Sam's things and move him to a hotel. After that, I only saw them again when Sam stopped by to say goodbye and pick up something he had left at my place by mistake.

I was devastated. I had cleared my entire weekend schedule, no small feat, to spend time with these guys, expecting we would all spend the weekend together. The problem was that I had never explicitly shared those expectations with them, and their weekend unfolded without me.

With an entire weekend free, I could have done any number of things, but I did nothing except wait to hear from them. It's a little humbling and embarrassing to write about how much self-created misery I experienced that weekend. Fully disconnected from Mental Freedom, I felt sorry for myself, dwelling on the idea that my friends just didn't care about me. Of course, that wasn't true, but it was the story in my head.

On Monday, after I pulled myself together, I realized there was something major I was supposed to learn from that painful situation. I wanted to find the GLOW, a concept I will unpack in chapter eight, "Appreciating the GLOW."

From that unnecessary pain, the Unconditional Trust Challenge was born. I realized that my friends were doing exactly what they were supposed to be doing to get what they wanted. I had arranged it, telling Sam he should come to spend time with Donny, never mentioning the idea that we should all spend time together. I had put myself through a weekend of torture, completely of my own making.

I decided to take on the Unconditional Trust Challenge for 30 days, and I was so happy with the results that it has become part of the Mental Freedom program. Since then, I have not had any other long-lasting painful experiences. I know how to convert pain into understanding and compassion, and now, when I get upset about something, it typically presents as a momentary twinge, never lasting longer than 15 minutes. With practice, you can accomplish this too.

Asking for What You Want

Participating in the Unconditional Trust Challenge should not prevent you from asking for what you want. You should absolutely let people know what you want in any relationship; just don't expect that you will get what you want just because you asked.

Some people will create opportunities for you to meet your needs within the context of the relationship you share with them, but it's not their responsibility to do so. If giving you what you want is what the other person wants to do, they will. However, if something is more important to them at the time, they may not. It is your responsibility to meet your needs, so instead of getting angry, decide from the following options: figure out how you can get what you want without their help, find a compromise that allows both of you to get what you each want or turn your focus to something else. Further, the Unconditional Trust Challenge does not involve putting up with harmful behavior.

Friends

Let's say that you were counting on your friend to go out to lunch with you, but they canceled because they decided they needed to clean their house instead.

You could feel resentful because your friend didn't prioritize their commitment to you; not only were you looking forward to sharing some news with your friend, but you were also really craving the menu item you planned to order. Whose problem is that? You might think it's your friend's problem—they're the one who broke their commitment—but upon deeper inspection, it should become clear that it's really *your* problem. You are the one who's most upset by it, you're the one who created the expectation, so the problem is yours—and therefore, it's yours to fix.

Instead of feeling frustrated, you could use the Unconditional Trust Challenge to remind yourself not to take it personally; your friend made the best choice for themselves at the time.

If you are involved with a person who rarely keeps their commitments, trust them to be someone who will likely bail on you. Further, you can create and communicate boundaries to protect yourself from feeling victimized repeatedly, or you can just stop asking them for things completely.

Accepting other people's choices doesn't mean you have to endorse or endure their thoughtless behavior. If their actions are egregious, you'll want to decide what kind of relationship you will have with them, if any. There are people in my life I no longer associate with because it's hard to watch them self-destruct. There are others who see the world so differently than I do that we have nothing in common anymore as a basis for friendship. (If you are reading this and thinking, "What if I can't leave? I know I have that choice but leaving goes against my value system, would be bad for the children, is a waste of all the time and energy I've invested into this relationship," there is something for you in the next chapter.)

Once you have fully accepted the people in your life for being who they've shown you they are, you have a decision to make about the extent of your relationship, if any—and you are 100% responsible for that choice.

Loved Ones

A friend of mine told me, "I used to worry about people I love; now I just love them."

Somehow, when we love someone, we believe it's our responsibility, our duty, to worry about them—but what if that's all wrong? What if the only responsibility we have to our loved ones is to love them?

Consider what your worrying communicates to the person being worried about. You might think it conveys love, but instead, it can be interpreted that you don't believe they are capable of handling the situation they are in. They may believe there is something wrong with them and that they can't continue without your approval. Or, on the other side, they may push ahead into risky territory just to prove to you that they can. Neither is what you would want for your loved one.

So often, people believe they have someone's best interests at heart while trying to change them into a "better" version of themselves. Although it may come from a place of love, how do you imagine those on the receiving end experience this? It frequently comes across as a criticism of the person they truly are, and they can grow resentful—or they can internalize the judgment and spiral even deeper into whatever worrying behaviors you were initially complaining about.

But are you really a good partner, sibling, parent, or friend if you don't worry about those you love? Holding onto this idea will surely compromise your Mental Freedom. You can choose to hold onto the worry and your attempts to help, fix, and over-care for those you love, but you will never have the joy of experiencing true Mental Freedom.

The best way to show you truly love someone is through unconditional trust. This isn't the brand of trust your parents used when they "trust" you won't have a party over the weekend while they are away, or your partner "trusts" you are where you say you are. In these cases, trust is emotional blackmail. "If I trust you and you don't follow through, then I can be justified in feeling angry or betrayed when you don't measure up."

When I love someone, I don't need to worry about them, because I trust they will do what's best for themselves—even when what they do is not best for me. This is the kind of trust the Unconditional Trust Challenge requires. If whatever they do doesn't work out the way they planned, I trust them to figure out their next best move. I also trust that if they want my help, they will ask me for it. Love doesn't need worry; love needs unconditional trust.

It may also help to remember that someone experiencing challenging times won't get much value from your worry and may even be harmed by it. Holding those you care about in compassion and unconditional trust will be so much more supportive and helpful.

You may accept the Unconditional Trust Challenge and still think a person you know is making a mistake—just remember that they may need something completely different than what you would need in a similar situation. What might be a disaster for you could be a success for someone else. Even if it's a painful choice, there are opportunities for growth and learning that can be positive. Just remember, you are the star and director of one show—yours. They get to direct and star in their own show, and you can decide to stick around as a supporting player.

Since deciding to take the challenge on, my life has presented multiple opportunities to practice. Whenever I find myself wanting someone in my life to make a different choice, I recognize it's time to apply the concept; I remind myself to trust them to do what's best and to learn from their mistakes, should they make any.

If you're ready, and even if you're not, take the Unconditional Trust Challenge with all the important people in your life for the next 30 days. You can renew your commitment any time you want.

Begin to accept that whatever other people do is their best effort to get what they want. If it's working for them, then you need to decide if what they are doing lines up with what you want in *your* life. Instead of trying to change them and their behavior, you can either be happy your loved one is getting what they want and supporting them, reach a negotiated solution where you are both satisfied with the outcome, or distance yourself and love them from afar.

If they are doing their best to get what they want and it isn't working for them, you might feel inclined to help. Remember, this is their journey, not yours. Sometimes people don't want help and need to figure it out for themselves.

I remember a mother speaking to me about her son doing things "the hard way," and I suggested that perhaps it wasn't the hard way for him—it was just *his* way. If your loved one is willing to accept your help, make sure you are being helpful based on your loved one's perception instead of judging or criticizing based on your own perception. It is best to simply provide some information they may not possess that will help them be more effective or make better decisions, if they choose to.

The same is true about your involvement in the relationship. When you take the Unconditional Trust Challenge, the proverbial ball is in your court. Always support someone for doing their best to get what they want before deciding how involved *you* want to be in the future of that relationship.

If you are ready, practice unconditional trust whenever you find yourself frustrated, hurt, angry, or disappointed by choices another person makes. Put trust in yourself and the Universe that everything will work out for your benefit, even if it doesn't seem that way initially. Let go of the desire to have others respond the way you want so you can be happy. Create your own happiness through the freedom and genuine love found in the Unconditional Trust Challenge.

Addiction

I don't believe anyone has the right to tell the people in their lives that they need to get sober. You can, however, let them know you wish that for them and would like it if they did. While it can be excruciating to watch the self-destruction and their desperate behaviors, you need to recognize that, ultimately, the decision is not yours. You don't have to like it, but to achieve Mental Freedom, you must accept that it's *their* life and they have the right, and the responsibility, to live it the way they think is best.

If you happen to love an addict and choose to accept their right to live their life the way they want to, it is your responsibility to consider what relationship you will share with them. You can enable their addiction, you can work on an intervention, you can love them without enabling them, you can love them from a distance, or you can cut them out of your life completely. You don't have a say in your loved one's behavior, other than to express your opinion, but how involved you'll be with them is 100% your choice.

Whatever decision you make, you need to make it based on what is best for you. It shouldn't be an attempt to get your loved one to stop using; that would mean you're using your relationship as leverage to get them to do what you think is best. It could be that they believe using is their only way to survive, and you can never know because you are not them.

You need to trust that they are doing their best to get what they want with the information available to them. Should you have information that could help them in their decision-making, seek their permission to share it. If granted, share what you know, but don't continue to nag them. Supply the information and back off. Sometimes people won't make the best decisions when feeling pressure from someone else. If they want to please you, they might acquiesce and do things your way. If they want to show they are their own person, they'll do the opposite of what you want. The best way to ensure people make the best decision for themselves is to keep your interests out of it.

An interesting result of practicing unconditional trust is that when you stop trying to change or "fix" the people in your life, they often begin to make better decisions. Many of their decisions and much of their behavior could be in response to your perceived judgment. When you start practicing unconditional trust, they become free to make the decisions that are best for *their* lives. Until then, they may be subconsciously responding to the criticism they perceive from you. Participate in the Unconditional Trust Challenge, give it enough time for your loved one to trust the change, and watch what happens.

Clarity

Another benefit of practicing the Unconditional Trust Challenge is that it becomes easy to achieve clarity when you are willing to recognize it. When you clearly see what a person is doing, you learn two critical things: what it is they want and the best behavior they have to get it.

With these realizations comes the understanding that it isn't personal. It's very rare that what someone wants is simply to cause you pain. People aren't trying to do things *to* you; they are doing things *for* themselves. People do what they do to get what *they* want, not to do something *to* you.

It also becomes clear that while everyone isn't making the right, best, or most moral decision, whatever they chose was the best option they had available to them. This allows you to feel compassion that they didn't have anything better. Being able to understand what a person wants will help you decide how you want to define the relationship moving forward. You can accept the small part of the person you aren't crazy about and let go of your frustration, draw some boundaries around the relationship, love them from a distance, or end the relationship.

As mentioned in the introduction to this chapter, the benefits that come with clarity are nonjudgment, compassion, and forgiveness. There is no need to judge someone who is doing their best. You can develop compassion for the fact that the behavior they used was the best they had, and forgiveness is the next logical step.

Forgiveness

Acceptance is the precursor to forgiveness; it's difficult to forgive something you haven't accepted. Acceptance doesn't mean you approve, and forgiveness doesn't mean you are willing to allow them to hurt you again. Forgiveness is what you do because you deserve peace, not because the other person deserves absolution. When it comes to forgiveness, I love the unattributed quote: "Holding a grudge is like drinking poison and expecting the other person to die." With the Unconditional Trust Challenge, there is no need to drink that poison.

Forgiveness doesn't mean you agree with what the person did. It simply means you trust that they did the best they could to get what they wanted, so there is no reason to hold a grudge. You forgive because it will enhance your Mental Freedom.

There are several ways to forgive: Believing the person has

changed, you can put the transgression behind you and move forward with a renewed relationship. Recognizing that they did the best they knew how to get what they wanted, you can let them know you forgive them for the pain of not meeting your expectations, but you prefer to end or restrict the relationship to protect yourself from further injury. Finally, you can extend the Unconditional Trust Challenge in your heart but never have another interaction with the person.

Choosing any of these options will stop you from continuing to poison yourself and will help you see the other person as they are, all while forgiving them and protecting yourself in the process.

The Secret Weapon of the Unconditional Trust Challenge

The best thing about the Unconditional Trust Challenge is that it applies to you, too. Most people have something from their past that they regret. Put yourself back in that situation, as the person you were then, and answer this question: Were you doing the very best you could to get what you wanted at that moment? You may not have considered that question before and feel you need time to think about your response, but I already know the answer—of course, you were!

When you can accept the truth of that, you might be able to extend nonjudgment, compassion, and forgiveness to that younger version of yourself. You deserve it. You are worthy of it. This can free you from the guilt and shame you have been heaping on yourself, ultimately leading to increased Mental Freedom.

We tend to judge our younger selves based on who we are today instead of who we were when we did the things we regret. You wouldn't do the same things today because you have developed better behaviors to get the things you want, and in many cases, you want different things now. It's unfair to judge your past behavior with your standards of today. You may think it will prevent you from making similar mistakes, but it often leads to the opposite. It tends to demoralize you, causing you to identify as someone who always makes bad decisions.

For greater Mental Freedom, use the Unconditional Trust Challenge with yourself. Everything you have ever done was the best you knew at the time to get what you wanted, and the same is true for anything you do in the future. Give yourself a break!

Final Considerations

I once had a client say that, to him, it seemed that the Unconditional Trust Challenge leads to complete freedom from others. When you have zero expectations of others and can take care of yourself, he thought you would become totally self-sufficient, no longer needing others.

It is true, you may no longer need others. This may sound very lonely, but it's not necessarily a bad thing. You might no longer need others, but you will still want others in your life. This is a much freer position to be in. Depending on your circumstances and how strongly you experience your need for Connection, you might have many people to choose from to spend time with, or it could mean that you are very comfortable doing things by yourself.

You may also be thinking, "Why do I have to practice the Unconditional Trust Challenge when other people in my life aren't?" First, no one *has* to do the Unconditional Trust Challenge. It's a choice. Secondly, it's part of the Mental Freedom Experience. If you want more Mental Freedom in your life, this is one way to get it. You are doing it for yourself, not for others. This is to make your life better.

If others don't want Mental Freedom for themselves, or they don't see its benefits, they won't pursue it. That shouldn't stop you from having more Mental Freedom in your life.

What if you have people in your life who love you but don't unconditionally trust you and expect certain things from you, and all you want is to just be yourself? Unfortunately, you can't make other people practice the Unconditional Trust Challenge. Remember, all the principles of Mental Freedom are for you only. Of course, you can share information with others, but you won't be able to force them to value this the same way you do. In fact, if you are truly practicing Mental Freedom, you wouldn't even think to do that.

You aren't in charge of other people's expectations; all you can do is become response-able. Decide what will get you the most of what you want: either meet their expectations, strike a middle ground, or go your own way.

When your job is to guide someone else's behavior—as a parent, teacher, or manager—don't punish them for doing their best. Instead, provide them with information that will help them do better in the future. Remember, what works for you might work for someone else, but then again, it may not. You are a different person with different knowledge, values, focus, beliefs, needs, and desires. For this reason, and for your own Mental Freedom, it's a good idea to avoid giving advice. Help guide the people in your life to find the decision that's best for them from their perspective, not yours.

Summary

1. Mental Freedom comes when you take the Unconditional Trust Challenge.
   a. Recognize everyone is doing their best to get what they want at any moment.
   b. Relinquish your expectations of others.
   c. Practice nonjudgment, compassion, and forgiveness.
   d. Take responsibility for your relationships once you have accepted this challenge.
2. Mental Freedom increases when you ask for what you want without expectations of getting it the way you want it.

3. Use the Unconditional Trust Challenge with yourself so you can learn from your past instead of regretting it.
4. Take the challenge for yourself. You can share it with others but don't expect them to value it the same way you do.

Free Your Mind

Empowering vs. Victimizing Language

"You don't have to. You get to." –Jess Sims

Fostering a conscious awareness of the language you use is one of the most effective ways to incorporate the concepts of Mental Freedom into your life. Language comprises many colloquialisms that are disempowering and victimizing, the opposite of Mental Freedom's effects and values. It's very likely that you repeat words or phrases without realizing that they're working to restrict you when you're trying to emerge free. Maintaining a state of awareness will allow you to truly hear the words you are thinking and speaking, and being conscious and cautious about the language you use will propel you on the path toward greater Mental Freedom.

For example, have you ever called yourself a failure? Did you ever label yourself a worthless idiot, or even worse? The way you talk to yourself is directed by your self-esteem, and it's difficult to like yourself while regularly speaking harshly about your very core. (My book, *Choosing Me Now*, helps people improve that all-important relationship with themselves.)

The words you say to yourself shape your reality. A person who is constantly complaining that they are bad luck invites more bad luck upon themselves. A person who announces they must be unlovable isolates themselves further from potential relationships. People abdicate degrees of their Mental Freedom whenever they use disempowering language—language that places the power outside of themselves and onto random events or other people.

Should and Must

Eliminate "should" and "must" from your vocabulary. When talking about yourself, these words cast you in a victim role, which will never help you feel more empowered. Use them when talking to others and you become self-righteous, believing you know what's best for them, and no one can know what is best for another person. You can look at someone's situation and share what you think you would do. However, you have different values, needs, behaviors, desires, and perceptions, so it's impossible for you to tell someone else what they should or shouldn't do with any degree of certainty. It's not for you to say; it's not your life. You won't have to live with the consequences of those choices; they will.

What you can do is connect what you think the person should do in a particular situation with something they want. For example, when I had sons in middle school who didn't want to shower, it would do me no good to tell them how often they should shower. I can't force them into the shower, and even if I could, I have no control over what they do in there. But when they started to like girls, a shower became more likely when I reminded them, "Girls might want to spend more time with you if you were cleaner." Because what I wanted from them coincided with something they wanted, this approach had greater success. In fact, before long, I had trouble getting them out of the shower.

If you are unable to connect what you want with something they want, then drop it.

"I Can't"

Whenever I'm helping a client achieve greater Mental Freedom and they say, "I can't," I like to respond with, "Well, you could, but you might not want to." It's important to stop boxing yourself in by limiting your options. The path to Mental Freedom requires you to expand your options, not limit them.

Another empowering way to address, "I can't" is with a trick by Carol Dweck's as described in her book, *Mindset*. When you catch yourself saying "I can't," add the word "yet" as a reminder that, if it's important enough, you can learn to do it.

"I Had No Choice"

This is an expression people use when they can't identify a choice that is preferable—but there are always choices, you just may not like your options.

Let's consider the worst scenario I can think of: Someone holds a gun to my head and wants me to do something I'd never choose on my own, but my choices are to comply or try to get away. Most people would comply because they believe complying will increase their odds of staying alive. Trying other alternatives like pleading or running might be more or less successful, but the choice is theirs to make. They are the ones who will live with the consequences.

There are always choices when you are willing to accept the consequences. You might not perceive any of the available choices to be good ones, and you might not want to pay the consequences, but there are always choices, and there's always something else you could try.

"I Had No Time"

Another phrase you'll want to pay attention to is, "I had no time." Practicing Mental Freedom requires taking personal responsibility for the choices you make. Therefore, it's not accurate to say, "I had no time," "I ran out of time," or "There just wasn't time to do it." These are all cop-outs. The correct and honest thing to say is, "I didn't prioritize it," or "I had other things I wanted to take care of."

This may seem harsh, but it has more integrity than, "I didn't have time." There may be reasons you choose not to take responsibility in this way, such as potential consequences that can harm the relationship, but understand it is the truth whether you express it or not.

Wants vs. Needs

Achieving Mental Freedom will require you to make the distinction between needs and wants. Chapter two, "What Motivates You," covered the five basic human needs that everyone is biologically driven to meet: Safety & Security, Connection, Significance, Freedom, and Joy. It is correct to say you *need* these five things, but everything else is something you want. While you have specific ideas of how you'd like to satisfy your needs, you can always find something else that will work if, for some reason, you can't have what you want.

You may want a car to get to and from work, but if you can't afford one, you can carpool, use public transportation, ride a bicycle, or walk. If none of those options are available or realistic, you can consider moving closer to your job or seeking employment elsewhere. You may be in love with someone who doesn't love you back. You don't *need* that person; you want them. Even without any love interest in your life, you can still share love with family, friends, and even pets. If you find yourself incarcerated, you may want nothing more than to be released, but this is highly unlikely. You can still meet your Freedom need by making choices while in prison. You choose who to associate with, what food you eat, and how you spend your time. Another source of Freedom is what you do with your mind; you are always free to think about whatever you wish. If what you want is to take a trip around the world, you may not be able to afford that, but you can still get your Joy need satisfied in any number of ways. Your idea of Safety & Security might be moving out of your neighborhood into a nice home with a security system. This may not be immediately available to you, but perhaps you can take a self-defense class.

It is disempowering to tell yourself that something you want is something you need. By doing so, you can create so much frustration and misery because telling yourself you need something subconsciously implies you're unable to survive without it, and that's not true. Believing you are being deprived of something you need is a drastically different experience than lacking something you want.

"How Can I Get Them to...?"

Starting a question with, "How can I get them to...?" is disempowering because you can't control people's behavior. Of course, it's possible that you can make the consequences for noncompliance so severe that people will choose to comply, but there will be no motivation to continue to do so once you are no longer present.

To live your life according to the principles of Mental Freedom, you must learn to accept how others choose to live their lives. That doesn't mean you have to approve of their choices, but you navigate your relationships with the understanding that you don't have the right to tell others what to do. Besides, when you're focused on the only thing you can control (yourself), you will be too busy living your own life to worry about what other people are doing.

Should someone ask you for your opinion, you can provide it, but make sure the person understands that you're sharing what is true for you—it may not apply to the way they want to live their life. You are two different people, after all. A more effective way to help is to first ask yourself, "How can I provide information that may lead to a different result?"

As a parent, teacher, counselor, or supervisor, you are responsible for the growth and development of others. To get a desired outcome from your child, student, client, or employee, you'll want to connect with their internal motivation. Behavior is motivated from the inside out; it is what drives us all to do what we do. If you don't believe that, try to get someone to do something they don't want to do when they don't care about the consequences you are threatening them with. It won't happen.

"They Made Me…"

No one has the power to *make* you do or feel anything. This statement is disempowering because it is you who is responsible for what you do, think, and feel. You can allow someone to influence your behavior and feelings, but it isn't a foregone conclusion. You always have the power to choose your response, even when the consequence of not complying is your life. In this extreme example, most people would certainly comply with the aggressor. It's true that this could require you to act in a way you would never choose yourself, but because you're motivated by your desire to live, you ultimately do want to choose to comply. However, if you are willing to pay the price of your life, even a person threatening to kill you couldn't *make* you do something you didn't want to do.

"Have To" vs. "Want To"

You can achieve great progress toward Mental Freedom by recognizing everything you do is because you ultimately want to. Many people complain about the things they *have* to do because they're ignoring the ultimate desire that motivates them through the mundane, dreadful, or even painful parts of life.

Make an effort to recognize how often you complain about things you *have* to do. The truth is there is only one thing you *have* to do, and that is eventually die one day. Until that moment, every other thing you do is because you *want* to. If you truly didn't want to do it, you wouldn't.

Believing you are being forced to do things by outside forces creates a lot of misery for you to carry. Nothing can make you do something against your will. Even if it is unpleasant, there will always be a reason why you chose to do it. Once you understand this, it becomes easy to accept full responsibility for every action you choose—the good and the bad. This is the path to power and freedom. You are in charge of your decisions, no one else is.

Many of you reading this probably think I'm crazy. There are so many things people genuinely believe they *have* to do: make the bed, take care of the kids, go to work, pay the bills, clean the house, cook dinner, do the laundry, visit sick Aunt Sally, mow the grass, and so on. But do you really *have* to do any of those things? If you are willing to pay the consequences, you don't *have* to do anything.

You don't *have* to make your bed. There may be reasons you prefer it made, but you really don't have to make it. When bedtime comes, you can still get into it unmade. You don't *have* to take care of your kids. When I worked in foster care, I knew several parents who tested that theory. If there aren't any relatives who will do that for you, governmental agencies will step in. You don't have to go to work or pay your bills. You could live homeless, become self-sufficient, or maybe live in a relative's basement. You really don't *have* to clean the house. It's possible to live in chaos and filth; it's also possible to hire someone else to clean the house. You don't *have* to cook dinner. You can pick at snacks, make sandwiches, go out to eat, or skip the meal entirely. You don't *have* to do the laundry. You could wear dirty clothes, buy new ones, or adopt a nudist lifestyle. You don't *have* to visit your sick aunt Sally. She's going to be sick whether you visit or not. You don't *have* to mow your yard. You can ignore it and let it grow wild.

Some of these probably sound like irresponsible choices. You might be thinking, "I would never live in my brother's basement!" or "I could never become a nudist!" But these ridiculous alternatives underline the importance of changing your internal and external language: Reframing your thinking from "I have to do it" to "I want to" or "I get to do it" will make a big difference in the amount of Mental Freedom you experience.

Scholars from Stanford write, "Studying how people use language—what words and phrases they unconsciously choose and combine—can help us better understand ourselves and why we behave the way we do." If we consciously choose and combine our words and phrases differently, we can change how we behave, which is a goal of Mental Freedom.

The next time you believe you *have* to do something, remember that you don't. To reframe your thinking into a "want to/get to" mindset, you need to discover your reason why. Why do you do those things you tell yourself you have to? There should be a compelling reason. Without one, you wouldn't do it, because you don't *have* to do anything.

Your Reason Why

Let's explore some possible reasons for doing each of those daily chores of living items mentioned above.

People generally *want* to make their bed because it makes their room look neat, or they want to keep things out like dust, pet hair, or bugs. People clean the house because they like living in a tidy environment. They cook dinner because they like to eat and want to nourish themselves and others. They take care of their children because they love them and want them to be healthy and safe. People visit their sick aunts because they want to show kindness and sympathy to a loved one who is hurting. They go to work to earn money to pay their bills, so they have a house to live in, a car to drive, and utility services.

When you stop telling yourself the things you do are because you *have* to and start living with the knowledge that you *want* to or *get* to do everything you choose, the entire experience changes.

Consider how heavy it feels going through life believing you do the things you do because you have no other choice—you *have* to, or you *must*. This fosters a victim mentality. Who wants to be a victim? I know I sure don't. Instead of saying, "I have to go to work and clean the house," you can empower yourself by shifting to, "I get to go to work and pay my bills to keep my house warm and well-lit, and I want to clean it so I can feel good about relaxing in it and having friends over."

People often resist this concept and argue with me, saying they won't go as far as saying they *want* to do the task but are willing to admit to at least *choosing* to do it. This can be an intermediary step, but it doesn't quite do the job of achieving Mental Freedom.

If Mental Freedom is your goal, you'll be able to identify

why you *want* to do the task—the boring chore of daily life, the monumental project at work, the dreadful responsibility with no end in sight—and truly believe it. When in doubt, revisit your reason: It is either to gain something you want or to avoid something you don't. If you can't find a good reason for doing something, then simply stop. If the reason you did something is no longer valid nor makes up for the inconvenience or pain of doing it, then find an alternative path to get what you want or stop entirely. If you're willing to pay the consequences for not doing something and are unable to discover a reason why you'd want to do it, then don't do it.

Mental Freedom requires you to abandon the victim role, take responsibility for your choices, evaluate the effectiveness of your choices along the way, and adjust them when it makes sense.

A friend of mine hated her job because of the person in charge, who had fired her sister without cause. She wanted to quit in solidarity with her sister, but she believed she *had* to stay. When I asked why, she explained that her husband's debilitating disease required a lot of medical care. As a part-time secretary receiving full-time benefits, she didn't believe she would ever find another full-time job with such great healthcare. She felt trapped. She had looked for other jobs with full-time benefits and found nothing. It was true that the arrangement she had was rare—especially considering that she really did enjoy her work and even got along with her coworkers.

When I asked what her reason for staying was, she talked about being able to get her husband the best healthcare available. I responded, "Then you really *do* want to work there to provide for your husband." She looked at me with her mouth agape and said, "I guess I really do."

I asked her to consider how it feels to wake up every day and drag herself out of bed while thinking, "I *have* to go to that job with that horrible woman." Then, I asked her to imagine waking up and thinking about how she *gets* to go to a job she likes, with coworkers she respects, that provides essential, high-quality care for her husband. The shift in mindset had an immediate effect, making her feel lighter and happier. She made the commitment to change her language, internally and externally.

This conversation took place in 1997, and she still works there, happily, today. She could have stopped halfway by accepting that she chooses to stay at the job she hates for her husband's sake, but that would only have unlocked the door of the mental prison she created for herself, potentially leading to her feeling resentment toward her husband. The simple but monumental shift from "have to" to "want to" did more than just unlock the door: It allowed her to fully escape that mental prison she trapped herself in every morning, dragging herself to work with a "have to" attitude.

Your Test

Humor me by placing yourself in this (thankfully) made-up situation, as it will reveal whether or not you fully understand this chapter:

You have a $50,000 ring on your finger. While you are out shopping, you go into the public restroom, and upon entering a stall, you notice the toilet is broken and full of waste—absolutely disgusting. When you turn to leave that stall, your uninsured diamond ring falls off your finger and into the toilet bowl.

In this contrived horror scenario, you can't leave the stall or ask for help. Here are your choices: Leave the ring behind or retrieve it from the bowl of human waste. Most people decide to retrieve their ring, sure, but this is the question that will confirm your understanding of this chapter: Do you *want* to put your hand in that toilet? If you answered "no," you don't yet understand the mindset shift needed to achieve Mental Freedom. The correct answer is yes, you *want* to put your hand in that toilet—you want to retrieve your ring.

Collectivistic Cultures

If you happen to be from a collectivistic culture, you may think the information in this chapter doesn't apply to you, but it does.

As someone in a collectivistic culture, you are encouraged to prioritize the good of the whole over the preferences of the individual. This places a strong emphasis on the responsibilities created by the need for Connection. The group can involve one's family, a work team, or a community. Taking care of the group you're responsible for seems like a definite "have to," but it isn't. It's true that you have been acculturated to put the needs of the group above your own, whether it's your family or community, but when applying Mental Freedom, it means that you want to choose to be response-able for them.

It still comes down to discovering your reason why. You could be taking care of your aging parents because you want to show them you love and respect them, bring happiness into their lives, or alleviate their suffering. Maybe you want to be the type of person who prioritizes family, or maybe it's because you feel like you owe them. When you're experiencing pressure related to family, it's especially important to ask yourself, "What kind of person do I want to be in this situation?" The answer to that question is your reason. Now, you can shift from "have to" to "want to."

If you don't have a good reason for what you're doing and are willing to pay the consequences, you could stop. When you obligate yourself to do something you don't want to do, you breed resentment, which is not healthy for your relationships with others or your relationship with Self.

It's possible to encounter a situation that feels as though you must choose between taking responsibility for someone else and your own Mental Freedom. Ask yourself, "How can I be a good parent, spouse, child, employee, or friend and still achieve Mental Freedom?" Make it a both/and instead of an either/or. With this mindset, you can redefine what being a good participant in the relationship looks like. The priority can't *always* be taking care of others; sometimes you need to address your own needs before you can be of service to those you love.

This concept of identifying your reason to shift from "have to" to "want to" can be even more crucial for those living in a collectivistic culture to understand. Otherwise, they run the risk of serving others from within that self-maintained mental prison created by the notion that they have no choice. You can find Mental Freedom when living in service to others if you are doing it because you want to. If you are struggling to find your reason why, an appointment with a Mental Freedom specialist can help.

Gratitude

Another tool for shifting from a "have to" to a "want to" mindset is linking your reason to gratitude. My friend who felt she had to keep her job with an awful boss can feel gratitude for receiving full-time healthcare benefits as a part-time employee. She can focus on how grateful she is that her husband is still alive, appreciating that it's because she goes to work and earns an excellent insurance policy. In the disgusting case of the ring in the toilet, the person can be grateful they have hands with which to retrieve their ring. They can be grateful that the ring is still within reach and wasn't flushed away. And afterward, they get to be grateful for soap and running water.

Instead of focusing on how annoying it can be to make the bed, you can be grateful you have a comfortable place to sleep with sheets, pillows, and blankets. Rather than stressing about cleaning your home, you can be grateful you have somewhere safe to live, full of lovely things you get to organize, arrange, and occasionally clean. Even if you feel like you're stuck *having* to clean after someone else, you can remember the reason why you actually *want* to clean a mess that isn't yours. While it might be a challenging next step, you can choose to focus on how grateful you are to have that person in your life.

An important consideration with gratitude is to not push people toward it. Before offering this concept to someone, it's important to assess their readiness. Someone who is deep in the experience of grief and loss may not be ready to focus on gratitude. Not only will they dig into feeling their pain but they also can get offended and distance themselves from you. Always be respectful of where a person is before trying to introduce the concept of gratitude. I might say something like, "I know you are in a very dark place right now, but when you are ready to feel better, an approach I have used to help me into the light is focusing on gratitude."

Affirmations

Another tool for shaping and clarifying your self-talk is affirmation—or "telling the truth in advance," as my good friend and colleague, Lamont Brown, likes to say.

Affirmations are extremely powerful, so you need to craft them deliberately to ensure you get the outcome you want. In his book, The Success Principles, Jack Canfield writes about nine elements of effective affirmations:

1. Affirmations begin with the two powerful words, "I am." You don't have the power to affirm things for others.

2. Use action words in the affirmation: learning, growing, earning, and loving, for example.

3. You will get exactly what you affirm, so be specific. I once had an affirmation that declared, "On Dec. 31, 2006, I have zero balances on my credit cards." I did have zero balances on my credit cards by then, but it was because I transferred those balances to a line of credit I had secured. I hadn't reduced my actual debt one bit.

4. Successful affirmations are brief and simple. Do not try to write an affirmation covering several things all at once.

5. Write them as positive statements, declaring what

you want to attain rather than what you are trying to avoid. Before I ever knew about the power of affirmations, I used to say, "Please God, whatever you do, don't let me be a single mother raising teenage boys alone." About 18 years later, I was a single mother raising teenage boys alone after my husband died. By affirming what I didn't want, I invited it by focusing on the idea of "a single mother raising teenage boys alone." A successful affirmation would have been, "My partner and I work together to raise children we are proud of."

6. Use present tense. If you use future tense, you are affirming that what you want will never happen. For example, "I will weigh 140 pounds by this date" equates to you *will* but never *do*. You want to declare them as if they are already happening.

7. You must affirm something for yourself. You can't affirm things for other people. Your power to attract what you need into your life only works for what *you* want.

8. Affirmations work best when you include a dynamic emotion. Using words such as happily, joyfully, amazingly, peacefully, or ecstatically in your affirmations will help you feel that emotion as you repeat them. It is the experience of the emotion that raises your energy vibration to attract your desired affirmation into your life.

9. Always end your affirmation with the phrase, "or something better," allowing for better-than-you-can-imagine outcomes manifesting in your life.

Example: I am excitedly marching toward Mental Freedom's success with all the people who support me, or something better.

Another good friend and Choice Theory colleague of mine, Bruce Davenport, says, "You will never change your life until you change something you do every day. The secret to improvement is found in your daily routine." Find a way to link your affirmations to a daily task, like eating lunch, brushing your teeth, waking up, or preparing to sleep.

Simply changing "have to" to "want to" will drastically influence the amount of Mental Freedom you can enjoy, but attending to all the suggestions in this chapter will further magnify those gains.

Believing you are being forced to do things by outside forces creates misery for yourself. Nothing can make you do something against your will. It may be unpleasant, but there will always be an internal reason or motivation for why you chose to do it. Accept that, own it, and be willing to take full responsibility for every action you choose—the good and the bad. This is the path to power and freedom. You are always in charge of your decisions; no one else is.

Summary

1. There are many colloquialisms that are disempowering and victimizing.

2. The words you use can shape your reality.

3. There are several phrases you can work on reducing or even eliminating from your vocabulary, starting with "have to," "need to," "should," and "must." Free yourself from this language by determining why you truly want to do the things you do.

4. Once you get in touch with your "why," you will never *have* to do another thing again. "You really *do* want to put your hand in that toilet to get your ring."

5. If you were raised in a collectivistic culture, you may believe you must subjugate what *you* want for what your family needs. You can make the choice to prioritize your own needs, but your cultural norms and values, along with the consequential societal consequences for putting yourself first, will likely cause you to *want* to prioritize your family.

6. Feeling gratitude for what you gain by doing the things you think you *have* to do will help shift your understanding to why you *want* to do them.

7. Affirmations are a technique for shaping your self-talk. Because of the extreme power affirmations can yield, remember to craft them according to Jack Canfield's nine guidelines.

Rewriting the Stories in Your Head

"Pain is inevitable. Suffering is optional." –Haruki Murakami

Our brains tend to fill in the blanks in situations where we believe we are missing important details. The only problem is that our brains fabricate this information we crave based on our best guess, and most of the time, that guess has nothing to do with what is best! At its worst, it is the act of catastrophizing.

Factors that Create Stories in Our Heads

We all create and host stories in our heads without any real evidence of their validity. Three factors play into this: the need for closure or patterns that make sense, the desire to know what motivates others, and the brain's hardwiring for negativity.

Needing closure. If you have ever gone to see a movie that left the ending to your imagination, then you know how frustrating it can be. We like to know how the story ends! The movie *Inception* had me wondering what was real and what was not, and I thought about the ending for days afterward, frustrated and uncertain.

The same is true in our lives. When something happens and we don't understand how it came to be, we try to explain it anyway. Unable to make a coherent, complete picture of a situation with limited information, we conjure up stories in an attempt to get closure.

Wanting to understand what motivates others. Chapter two, "What Motivates You," covered the concept that behavior is always internally motivated by something a person wants, which is dictated by the satisfaction level of the needs: Safety & Security, Connection, Significance, Freedom, and Joy. Chapter four, "The Unconditional Trust Challenge," underlined how this concept means other people's behavior should rarely be taken personally.

The people in our lives can do things that make no sense to us, causing our minds to go into overdrive to find an acceptable explanation. The final factor below explains why we usually generate an explanation that is hurtful.

The human brain's negativity bias. Evolution hardwired our brains this way to protect us. Back when humans were nomadic hunter-gatherers, they needed to notice the slightest change to their environment as it could have made the difference between life and death—and the ones who noticed survived, solidifying the hardwiring for negativity through the centuries.

For example, the sudden silence of birds could indicate a nearby predator. A distant snap in the woods could be the sound of an approaching stranger. A large group of animals grazing in a field could mean a storm was rolling in.

Soldiers in combat zones are trained to develop this hardwiring further; they want to heighten this negativity bias because, once again, it could mean life or death. For them, anything amiss could mean an attack is imminent. These situations require people to rely on the brain's default wiring for negativity.

However, if you are reading this book, it is likely you are not being hunted, you have shelter from storms, and you are not living in a combat zone. Even still, your brain tries to keep you safe with its negativity bias.

The path to Mental Freedom teaches you to wire your own positive pathways to coexist alongside the innate negative wiring so you can still protect yourself, but you can also increase your Mental Freedom.

Self-Created Misery

Combine the tendency to make up entirely fabricated stories without evidence with the brain's hardwiring for negativity and you are in for some self-created misery. If you are attempting to create understanding and find closure, negativity bias will direct you to fabricate painful stories, which can have a devastating effect on your Mental Freedom.

Have you ever walked into a room where other people were talking, and upon noticing you, they immediately stopped? You probably told yourself they were talking trash about you, but what evidence do you have to support that idea? Absolutely none. The story you created is simply a product of negativity bias.

The following scenarios depict how self-created misery can take root when people surrender to their negativity bias.

> Rachel has been in an exclusive relationship for a year. One day, she is in a happy-ever-after relationship, and the next, her partner breaks up with her without explanation. Facing a big knowledge gap, she thinks to herself, "What happened? Why did he leave? We were so happy together! How did I not see that coming?"

The answers come hard and fast: "What happened?" *You are such a loser; your partner could not be around you anymore. They are probably involved with someone new already!* "Why did he leave?" *Is it not obvious? You are just not good enough. You talk too much, you don't talk enough, you are not pretty enough, you are too pretty, you don't make enough money, you make too much money, you are overweight, you are too skinny, you are just not sexy enough or you are too sexy. In fact, there is something so wrong with you that you are unlovable. No one will ever love you again.* "We were so happy together!" *Yeah, how oblivious can you be? You are floating around thinking you are in this great relationship, and the whole time, he was looking for a way out. He was probably cheating on you and you did not even know.* "How did I not see this coming?" *You are so trusting, it's ridiculous! You constantly make excuses and look the other way when you should be asking questions and paying closer attention. It is all your fault you are alone again.*

Posing questions like this causes your brain to search for answers, and in the absence of information, it will compose a fictional story about what might have happened. Using its default wiring, your brain is going to compose a story that is painful, and when your brain responds to your questions in this way, how do you think it leaves you feeling? That is right—horrible.

Tom is waiting for his wife, Amy, to get home from work; she is late and is not answering his calls. He begins to create the narrative that she must have been in a car accident. As the situation persists, he is terrified, imagining her dead along the roadside. He has zero evidence to support this story, but his mind is seeking an answer for Amy's unusual behavior, and negativity bias delivers the worst-case scenario.

In situations of panic, the mind can conjure up terrible ideas, and even when a thought attempts to reassure you ("It is probably nothing, maybe her phone is dead,") fear can settle back in. While focused on the fear, it's difficult to stop the negative thinking. In fact, that is often the problem. Instead of telling yourself to stop worrying, plan your next dream vacation, write out your grocery list, solve a puzzle—anything that will take your mind somewhere else.

Logan is concerned because his husband, Anthony, has not been interested in sex and has been preoccupied for several days. He tells himself the story that Anthony must be having an affair. Why else would not he want to be intimate? He has no evidence to back up this suspicion; it's his negativity bias creating a painful scenario.

Feelings like hurt and anger can cause you to resist other explanations. This can be challenging because you want to trust your partner, but you also don't want to be taken by surprise or disregard your instincts. This is a good time to ask yourself, "What kind of person do I want to be in this situation? Do I want to be suspicious, non-trusting, and insecure, or do I want to be trusting, secure, and unconcerned?" That choice is always yours, but one leads you toward Mental Freedom and the other destroys it. Someone else's dishonesty does not define you. Take responsibility for your part of the relationship and relinquish responsibility for theirs by aligning yourself with your vision of the partner you want to be.

When your brain answers questions with painful stories, the only conclusion is feeling terrible. Even though the intention is to keep you emotionally safe by preparing you for the worst-case scenario, allowing your brain to jump to conclusions takes away from your Mental Freedom and can potentially harm your relationships. Instead, you can learn to work *with* it rather than let it run rampant, taking over your thinking processes.

The next time you encounter something that fills you with questions, pay attention to the voice that answers. Sometimes the voice is yours; sometimes it belongs to someone else—a parent or other relative, teacher, religious leader, current partner, an ex, or anyone from your past. Sometimes you hear the voice, and other times, you would not. Sometimes it whispers; sometimes it screams. When you allow that voice to continue unchecked, it wreaks havoc. Paying attention will help you determine whether or not you should continue to listen.

Do not spend energy battling with the voice; that gives it too much power and importance. The voice is not your enemy. In fact, it's something we all have that works to keep us safe. Be gentle with it, but remind it that things are not always as bad as they seem.

What Else Could Be True?

The first thing you need to do is recognize these stories as the fabrications they are. Not based on facts, the stories exist because you have encountered missing information. Your brain's hardwiring for negativity makes hurtful stories more likely than those that help you feel better. Once you recognize the negativity bias influencing your narrative, you can ask yourself the question, "What else could be true?"

If people immediately stop talking once you walk into a room, it's likely your brain will offer the idea that they must have been talking badly about you. Instead of latching onto that thought, question it. Is it really the only explanation?

Shifting to a more positive outlook, you might consider the possibility that it was just a private and extremely personal conversation. Perhaps someone had just confessed to something serious, or maybe they were discussing something embarrassing. This shifts your perspective from a negative narrative—they were talking about me—to a neutral one—someone has a secret that has nothing to do with me. Is this fabrication true? You may never know, just like you will never know if they were talking about you. Choose to believe the version helps you feel better. (It is the one about the secret, right?)

You can stretch your imagination further by creating a story that makes you feel terrific. Maybe they stopped talking because there is a big, beautiful surprise coming your way and they did not want to ruin it for you. Could that be true? Anything is possible.

In the example of Rachel's sudden breakup, the painful narrative claims her partner did not think she was good enough for him. If she decides to believe this heartbreaking story, she can decide to wallow in that terrible feeling or move on to the next step, which would be to examine her role in the relationship. If she is able to pinpoint things about herself she would like to improve upon, lesson learned. She could implement the changes she wants to make—not to get her ex back, but to be a better partner in her next relationship.

A neutral story for Rachel could involve her deciding to accept that not all relationships last, feel grateful for the time they shared, and look forward to what is next. There are often positive and negative aspects that balance out to a neutral story.

Shifting to a positive narrative, Rachel could choose to feel grateful she no longer has to spend time with someone who was not right for her. The "right person" would value her for what she brings to the relationship. She could tell herself that her partner had to leave because she was so wonderful; he did not deserve her and felt inadequate in her presence.

Once you have gained some distance from your unpleasant story, it's important to reflect and examine the situation to determine what you need to take responsibility for and how you can be response-able. Taking control of the made-up stories you tell yourself is a tool meant to free you from being held hostage by agonizing emotions. It is not to suggest that you should avoid taking inventory of how you contributed to the situation—in this case, the end of a relationship.

If you are doing it correctly, taking inventory of your responsibility in any situation won't cause you to feel bad. It is *not* about blaming yourself and creating more pain. It is about taking responsibility for your part in whatever occurred so you can stop feeling like the victim, gain more effective control, and achieve greater Mental Freedom. You want to examine your contribution so you can grow and do better next time. An unexamined life will lead to you repeating the same patterns.

In the example of Tom and Amy, Tom could assure himself that something must be delaying her rather than jumping to the conclusion that she may have been in an accident or dead. This is not to say that Amy was not in an accident; it is a possibility. However, spending time dwelling on the worst-case scenario has no effect on the outcome of a situation. If the worst was true, he would be notified soon enough. Tom allowing that story to take root in his head in the meantime only creates worry, anxiety, and stress, which are detrimental to his Mental Freedom and his health.

This is how I calmed my negativity bias when my son, Kyle, was serving in Iraq. If he were hurt or killed, I knew he would have died doing something he loved and that I would eventually be notified. Being unaware for that period of time would have been a gift. While he was deployed, this saved me from wallowing in anxiety and worry, granting me more Mental Freedom.

In the example with Logan and Anthony, Logan could tell himself a neutral story: Anthony must have something distracting on his mind that he will share whenever he is ready, or he will work it out himself without sharing. For a positive story, Logan could choose to believe that it must be a promotion Anthony is working hard to get to provide more money for their future together. Again, Logan's initial thought of infidelity is still a possibility. It is just that there is no sense in him ruminating on that narrative until he has more information to support that story.

My Painful Story

The first two years after my husband died were particularly difficult. Kyle was 13 years old at the time and took his father's death particularly hard. He believed his father was going to prove everyone wrong, especially the doctors, and recover from his illness. That did not happen.

Kyle went to counseling for a while, but he did not seem to get much out of it. He was grieving, and most of the time, his grief took the form of anger.

I would come home from work and say, "Hi, Kyle." He would respond with a venomous, "Screw you!" I told myself that my son must hate me—an excruciating story for me to believe, as I wanted nothing other than to help him work through his grief, but he was using me as a punching bag.

On good days, I could tell myself a neutral story: Kyle was in so much pain from the death of his father that he had to take it out on someone. Since he trusted me to never leave him, it was easiest to focus his anger and pain on me. But often, the story that my son hated me was prominent. It probably lasted a year and a half, until one day when I was scared he might hurt himself. I tried to restrain him on the floor with my arms and legs wrapped around him. Although he was a wrestler who could easily break free, he struggled some but did not really try to get away. I asked him why he hated me so much. He replied, "Mom, I don't hate you."

The damage that story did to me was so encompassing, and with those words, it was suddenly over. I recognized I had given in to my negativity bias, telling myself the most hurtful story to make sense of the situation. It was quite a relief, accompanied by a big dose of Mental Freedom, when I was finally able to release it.

I'm happy to report that Kyle is now 38 years old and a wonderful father to four remarkable children. I could not be prouder of the man he has become. Losing his father was hard, but it was the path he had to walk.

Writing Your New Story

Rewriting your story can require different things. Sometimes, you need to change your focus to find gratitude. Other times, it's about uncovering and facing your subconscious sabotage.

Changing your focus can be a challenge, especially when it's about scarcity versus abundance—focusing more on what you don't have instead of what you do, or what you can't do instead of what you can. This is a common experience.

This is exactly what I did in 2014 after breaking both of my ankles in a hot air balloon accident. Lying in a hospital bed far from home, I started to feel sorry for myself. Not only could I not walk but I was also missing my son's birthday, my grandson's baptism, and Thanksgiving with my family. Then I remembered that my family had just gotten 10 inches of snow and I was in Sedona, AZ, with a beautiful view of the mountains from my room, and I could roll myself outside in my wheelchair and sit in sunny, 80-degree weather. When I was thinking about not being able to walk, I remembered a time in 1983 when I went roller skating with my friend, Kathy. She fell, broke both her elbows, and received two hard casts with her elbows bent at 45-degree angles. She was unable to blow her nose, feed herself, or wipe her own behind. I felt a surge of gratitude knowing that I could do all those things. I was also grateful that my inability to walk was a temporary condition.

Being mindful—the active, open attention to the present moment—helps with remembering the things you *can* do and the things you *have* in your life. You can choose to recall what you can't do and what you don't have, or you can recount all the things you can still do and the things you do have. The former will generate pain while the latter can create satisfaction and contentment.

Finding Gratitude

After my husband died, I told myself I would never find anyone to love me again. Valentine's Day was the hardest holiday to get through—not because my husband was the romantic type, but because I had to endure all the commercialism telling me to buy this for the person I love, do this with the person I love, but I was convinced I was all alone. February 14 became my annual pity party. Even my boys had dates, so I was free to sit home alone, feeling sorry for myself.

After about three years of this, I remembered that I knew how to combat sad, angry, and anxious feelings: I had to either change what I was thinking or what I was doing. I still stayed home by myself, but I spent the day writing thank-you notes to the men in my life who helped me with my boys during our time of grief. There were many—from teachers, administrators, and coaches to my dad, brothers, brothers-in-law, friends, and community members. There were so many people to write to that it took me through the evening. I had written more than 100 thank-you notes, each with an individualized, personal message, and I was filled with such overwhelming gratitude and love. In fact, I felt more love that day than any other in recent memory, and I have not had another bad Valentine's Day again.

I did this for myself because I did not want to be sad on Valentine's Day, so I had not anticipated how helpful they would be for the people I had written them to. The response from them was amazing. It is not often you get to learn how you have helped others, people don't always communicate it, but many shared with me that they really needed my message of appreciation exactly at that time.

During disturbing times in your life, connecting with gratitude will propel you to a better place.

Uncovering Your Subconscious Sabotage

Have you ever had a goal you desperately wanted to reach, had the skills and support to get there, but just could not seem to make it happen? You may have been suffering from conscious or subconscious sabotage.

Sabotage is commonly defined as deliberately destroying, damaging, or obstructing something. Often occurring without your awareness, self-sabotage happens when you cannot get out of your own way to accomplish the things you really want to do. Some common areas of self-sabotage include finances, career advancement, relationship satisfaction, and overall happiness. It represents a lot of the work I do with my clients.

The Big Leap by Gay Hendricks proposes four main types of self-sabotage, and each is a different made-up story:

1. There is something wrong with me and I do not deserve this.

2. If I succeed, I will have to leave the people I care about behind.

3. When I accomplish what I want, I will have even bigger problems.

4. If I become successful, I will outshine someone important to me, and I don't want to hurt them like that.

Perhaps you recognize your use of these stories in your own life. They could be preventing you from achieving the success you crave.

Once again, there is usually no evidence to support these fabrications. When you engage in this kind of sabotage, you understand you have goals and recognize your ability to succeed, but for some unknown reason, you just cannot cross the finish line. This generally translates to a conflict between your conscious goals and things you subconsciously don't want to happen on your way to success. Take time to reflect and identify the stories you tell yourself so you can evaluate their veracity.

When you pull these stories from your subconscious and expose them in the light, you can determine if there is any truth to them. If not, you can archive them. If you do find truth, then you can decide what you want to do about it because you finally see it for what it is.

When I'm helping clients uncover their subconscious sabotage, I like to have them relax before asking them, "What would you have to give up to get what you want?" When relaxed, the mind will allow the answer to appear. It is typically experienced as a surprise, something that just pops into the person's mind. If you ask yourself that question, pay attention to the very first thought that jumps into your head. This is often the thing you are scared of.

Finances

When I started my business, I succeeded, doubling my income three years in a row. However, after the third year, I never doubled my income again, and in fact, I had a difficult time breaking through the high of that third year. I recognized that I must have been telling myself a story that was holding me back, and after some reflection, I discovered it.

My father had been a serial entrepreneur his whole life, quickly losing interest in what he was doing and moving on to his next big idea. He often just shut the business down without taking the time to sell it, so he never really became as successful as he hoped he would. My intentional contemplation revealed I was worried that if I became more successful than he was, he would not love me anymore. Was this true? Of course not, but I had been operating under that false assumption for quite some time. I was also worried about hurting him if I outshined him, but of course, he would be proud of me rather than feeling sorry for himself. Once revealed, the stories were dispelled, and my income began to increase as I was no longer trapped under the ceiling I had made for myself.

Job Advancement

I was working with a highly capable man, let us call him Greg, who wanted to be a coach. He was experienced in the field, had created his own materials and processes, and was already successful in running a nonprofit organization. He had everything he needed to retire from that and launch his coaching career, but he just would not move forward. When I asked him to settle down, relax, and consider what he would have to give up to achieve his goal, he was shocked by his answer: "My dream."

If he was successful, he would no longer have a dream to strive for—this was causing him to avoid the finish line. Of course, when he brought that into the light, he was able to see that he would be living his dream, reaching contentment, or creating room to consider what might be next. Once he was a successful coach, he decided to progress his career and work toward creating his own coach certification based on his own ideas and materials.

He was experiencing a version of, "If I succeed, I will have to leave the people I care about behind." He believed that if he succeeded, he would have to leave his dream behind.

Relationship Satisfaction

Sarah and Jaime were married, but it was not working out. Jaime filed for divorce and told Sarah she better get her act together, declaring she was so broken that she would break anyone she encountered. Sarah heard this, took it to heart, and moved to a new town. For six years, she kept her distance from others and avoided making friends, except for acquaintances at work. She did not even consider dating.

Sarah was one of the early participants in the Mental Freedom Experience, and when she was exposed to the material in this chapter, tears fell down her face. When asked what she was thinking, she shared what Jaime had said. She recognized that she had taken Jaime's story, believed it, and made it her own. It was not her who was broken; it was Jaime. Her self-sabotaging was a version of, "When I accomplish what I want, I will have even bigger problems." She believed that she would destroy anyone she started a relationship with.

She vowed to start living her life again, abandoning the belief that she was only capable of hurting others. It gave her more Mental Freedom than she ever thought possible.

Overall Happiness

When Wayne was young, his mother told him he was just like his father and would never amount to anything. Adopting his mother's story as his own, Wayne never made many friends—until he moved away from home to go to college, where he developed a robust social life. He even had an amazing girlfriend, Juanita, who loved him, and he loved her, too. But when he started to feel like things were too good to be true, his sabotaging belief altered his behavior: "There is something wrong with me and I do not deserve this."

Consistent with that belief, Wayne created a situation where Juanita would discover him in the arms of another woman. Devastated, she ended their relationship. While it was devastating for Wayne, too, he felt victorious for having control over the relationship ending, because that story in his head would not allow him to trust Juanita's feelings for him.

Tools to Help Rewrite the Narratives

Before rewriting your negative narrative, it helps to figure out how the distressing story served you. Even though it may no longer be serving you, when it began, it most likely provided benefits. I find these upsetting stories are often protective, keeping you from doing something that could cause even more pain—at the cost of keeping you from experiencing profound happiness.

When you decide to rewrite your story, you will have many tools at your disposal. You will want to create a story that you can imagine coming true. If your tale is so fantastical that it sounds like a joke to you, your brain won't be able to seriously imagine it, and you won't make any progress.

For example, it would have been too drastic of a change for Wayne to tell himself that everyone he met loved him, he would never believe that, but he might believe that he was loveable if he was able to love himself first. Greg's story did not allow him to start his coaching career because he was afraid of a life without hope. Once he recognized that achieving his dream would add to his life rather than subtract from it, he was able to move forward and start a highly successful coaching business.

Making up a hurtful story is an attempt to make sense of things that are uncertain, often giving you false hope that preparing for the worst will make it easier when it comes. That is simply not true. Wayne did not just anticipate the worst; he made it happen. Losing Juanita was unnecessary and far more painful than it would have been to discover and dismantle the stories in his head.

Another way these dire narratives can benefit you is by sharing them with others. When you do that, you are usually comforted by those you tell as they help convince you what you are thinking must be wrong, providing you with a false sense of security. Taking responsibility for your own Mental Freedom, you alone tell yourself better narratives and take control of creating your own happiness. There is no reason why you can't make up a story that serves you better, unless you are deliberately holding onto the excruciating story to get something you want—which you can do, by the way. You can hold onto the stories that create sadness, anxiety, or anger; no one has the power to make you relinquish them if you believe holding onto them is your best option.

Once the function of the original story is revealed, you will be able to choose other ways to serve that same function. You might even decide you no longer need that function, like what happened with Sarah. She held onto her story because she did not want to cause anyone else pain, but once she realized that story was not true, she easily let it go, and it flew away like a helium balloon.

The story you tell yourself should be proactive rather than a declaration that you will simply stop doing something. "I will stop doing" plans don't work. Instead, go one step further and spell out what it is you will do—not what you are going to stop doing. Neuroscience teaches us that we must replace old habits with new ones to create new neural pathways. It would not have helped me to change my story to, "I have to stop thinking about my dad when I'm making money." That maintains the idea that he would be jealous. Instead, I changed my story to, "Even though my dad was not as successful as he hoped to be, I know he is proud of what I'm doing with my business."

Visualization is another tool in your arsenal. Involve all of your senses and tune into your mind's eye to imagine what you will see, hear, smell, taste, and feel. Describing a full sensory experience can strengthen your engagement in your new story. If visualization doesn't come easy for you, try writing out the visualization and record yourself reading it so you can listen as you visualize. This is something I do because I'm not great at visualizing without an auditory component.

Do not leave this new story to chance. Tell yourself the new story several times a day so it becomes your go-to habit, and remember to be grateful for the outcome of the story even before it happens. Imagine it as if it's already true and express how grateful you are for it.

NINE STEPS TO CHANGE YOUR STORY

No matter how your mind holds you hostage, there is a way out. While it's important not to dismiss or deny your feelings, you can feel better once you decide you are ready to move forward and achieve Mental Freedom. Here is the process I have found effective in my own life and professionally with my clients:

1. Notice when you are experiencing something challenging like sadness, anger, or fear.
2. Find the word that best describes the feeling and

label your emotion—maybe it's devastation, fury, or concern.

3. Pinpoint where you are feeling it in your body and focus on releasing that sensation. Some people feel it in their temples, their solar plexus, their shoulders, their lower back, or their intestinal area.

4. Notice the thoughts that preceded the emotion you have labeled and connected to the physiological feeling. When you experience an emotion, you have thoughts that are typically consistent with that emotion. If your first instinct is to blame other people for how you are feeling, remember that emotions do not come from the outside—they are created by our own thoughts.

5. When you become aware of your thoughts, consider if they are true. The idea that someone else or some experience is "making you feel" whatever emotion you are experiencing can immediately be dismissed. External forces can't *make* you feel anything. You generate your emotions in response to thoughts you have about what is happening in your world. You can choose to generate other responses once you learn how, and that process will be the focus of the next chapter.

6. Recognize that your thoughts come from a story you made up that is not necessarily true. You probably don't have any hard evidence one way or the other, and you likely have no definitive way of ascertaining its authenticity.

7. If there is evidence to your hurtful story, consider whether it's definitive or if there could be other possible explanations. Ask yourself what else could be true.

8. Determine if you truly want to feel better. There is

often a benefit to staying in a victim role, and if you want to continue feeling this way, just keep telling yourself the same story.

9. If you want to feel better, take control as the author of your story: Whenever you want, you can tear it up and write a new one that creates better emotions.

IMAGINE NOT NEEDING AN EMOTIONAL STORY AT ALL

Elevating negative narratives into stories that are neutral or positive is a great achievement. However, there is another step you could take for a truly solid landing in the Mental Freedom arena: not needing an emotional story at all.

Everyone can achieve Mental Freedom, but they need to want it more than wanting to control everything that is happening in their life. Authentic Mental Freedom comes from taking the present moment exactly as it offers itself—no narratives, just acceptance. Stop judging the experience as good or bad, right or wrong, happy or sad. Recognize that it just is. I like to remind myself of Murakami's quote at the beginning of this chapter: "Pain is inevitable. Suffering is optional."

With enough experience making up stories that create positive emotions instead of negative ones, you can begin asking yourself, "Do I really need a story at all?"

Something happens as you undergo the process of liberating yourself from your mental prison: You become strong enough to simply accept what is happening without telling yourself a story about people and situations in your life.

You will know you are resisting when the story in your head sounds anything like, "It is not fair, "It was not supposed to be like this," "You broke your promise," "This is not right," "It should not have happened that way," or "Why did this happen to me?" All these statements represent your resistance to what already is. Your best course of action is accepting reality instead of beating your head against a brick wall trying to change it. Resisting reality is choosing to experience the pain of not having the world line up the way you want it, which is difficult enough. There is no reason to keep banging your head against that wall; it just creates more pain.

Whenever I experience the pain of reality not manifesting the way I want it to, I remind myself of my mantra of the year for 2021: "Nothing happens *to* me; everything happens *for* me." It is a much easier way to live. Whenever I recognize a distressing narrative, I switch to my mantra, and it lets me accept each moment as it comes without feeling the need to make up a story about it.

In December of that year, I was supposed to go to Singapore for some Choice Theory training. Singapore was strict with pandemic precautions, and I needed a negative test result no more than two days before flying. On the day of my flight, I still hadn't received the results. Thinking my results would come while I was in the airport, I tried to get on the plane, but they did not come until two hours after takeoff. I was not able to board that plane, but I reminded myself that "nothing happens to me, everything happens for me" and got a hotel room for the night before driving to my son's home a few hours away.

Because of the time difference, I ended up doing the training over Zoom in the middle of the night, which was challenging enough. Then, on the second day of the training session, I tested positive for Covid. I successfully completed the training while quarantined in a single room at my son's house. I frequently had to mute myself because I was coughing so hard, but I was able to complete the program.

Had I flown to Singapore and tested positive upon landing, I would have been quarantined for at least two weeks. Without my mantra, I would have been devastated about missing my flight. Even though I had no idea how it would work for me, I was able to let go of labeling it as a bad or disappointing circumstance. This makes space for the high probability that things are unfolding exactly the way they are supposed to for my highest good and the highest good of others. Not only does this solidify my belief in a benevolent Universe but it also allows me to not stress about anything that happens in my life.

A Chinese Proverb I have heard many times, "Maybe So, Maybe Not. We'll See," describes a series of seemingly unfortunate events that befall a farmer and his son, starting with their horse running away. The neighbors cry, "Terrible luck!" But the farmer says, "Maybe so, maybe not. We'll see." When the horse returns, it brings wild mares along with it. The neighbors shout, "Good for you!" And the farmer says, "Maybe so, maybe not. We'll see." Then, the farmer's son breaks his leg trying to tame one of the mares, and the neighbors shout, "How awful!" And the farmer says, "Maybe so, maybe not. We'll see." Weeks later, soldiers arrive in town to recruit able-bodied men for the army, choosing to leave the broken-legged boy behind. The neighbors rejoice, "Amazing, your son was spared!" And the farmer responds with the same: "Maybe so, maybe not. We'll see."

Life happens. We can tell ourselves stories—but do we really need to? There is no way to know how things will turn out, so rather than relying on a fabricated story to comfort ourselves, would it not be freeing to accept everything that comes our way with curiosity about what comes next?

Summary:

1. Humans have a need for closure. When we don't get that externally, we will make up our own story to create that closure.

2. Because humans are hardwired for negativity, we tend to make up the most excruciating stories we can imagine and believe them without any supporting evidence. Since we are not privy to the private thoughts of others, we also make up hurtful stories about why the people in our lives do the things they do.

3. Once you recognize the story you have been telling

yourself, you can take responsibility by examining its truthfulness. You will often find there is not any.

4. Follow this guidance when rewriting your story:
    a. Change your focus from scarcity to abundance—from what you can't do to what you can do, from what you don't have to what you do have.
    b. Discover what you are grateful for in the situation.
    c. Identify and dismantle your subconscious sabotage.
    d. Determine whether your new story is something you can truly believe.
    e. Consider what function your story served in the past and whether you want to maintain that function.
    f. Create a plan about what you are going to do instead of what you intend to stop doing.
    g. Involve all five of your senses to visualize your new story several times a day.

5. Complete the nine-step process for rewriting your painful stories.

6. Enhanced Mental Freedom can be achieved by remembering to accept what is happening without judgment. Relinquish control and trust that things are unfolding as they should.

Transform Your Life

Signals vs. Solutions

"It is almost impossible for anyone, even the most ineffective among us, to continue to choose misery after becoming aware that it is a choice." –William Glasser

The energy of the universe cannot be created or destroyed; it simply changes form.

This concept is called the first law of thermodynamics, and applied to Mental Freedom, it describes how we consider emotions and physical pain that doesn't have a medical cause. Emotions are energy moving through your body, and without the ability to transform them, they will remain. You either purge your emotions through expression or stuff them down, denying them rather than transforming them.

Emotions are seen as mysterious, unpredictable, and hard to ignore. Some schools of psychology believe studying our emotions will provide insight into why people do what they do. In Mental Freedom, we view emotions as information that helps us know if our life is the way we want it to be, experienced as satisfaction or happiness, or if something is not the way we want it to be, experienced as pain. This pain can result in sadness, anger, anxiety, or physical ailments without medical causes.

There are people who consciously manipulate others by faking or exaggerating their pain, and there are those with legitimate pain, like a broken bone, illness, or disease. However, there is something in between. The subconscious has the ability to protect us from experiencing painful emotions by converting it into physical pain—pain that is genuine and can be quite debilitating. It is so painful, in fact, that people find it difficult to believe there is not anything medically wrong with them as they experience headaches, backaches, joint pain, autoimmune disorders—conditions that couldn't possibly be created by their own brains. Who would want to needlessly experience such physical pain?

A person in this situation is not pretending. Their pain is real but there is no medical reason for it. For the rest of this chapter, when I refer to pain, it encompasses emotional pain as well as physical pain without biological causes.

Before applying the information in this chapter, address any physical pain with a healthcare provider to determine if you're experiencing a medical issue.

Pain begins as a signal that something is wrong, a warning that brings attention to a problem. When people ignore or hold onto pain, at some point, they recognize its benefits on a subconscious level. All they can feel is the excruciating, debilitating pain while being completely unaware of how it benefits them. Nonetheless, the brain registers those benefits, and without the knowledge and skills to achieve them in healthier ways, pain becomes the solution to a problem people do not even realize they have. The subconscious continues to create this pain long after it has served its original purpose.

This chapter is about how to help you recognize when you're using your pain to try to solve a problem you're experiencing so you can create a different behavior that allows you to get those benefits, and even more, in a way that allows you to relinquish the pain.

It is with extreme sensitivity that I write this chapter. I don't intend to blame you for your pain; I want to help you recognize if your pain is being used as a solution to a problem. The next chapter presents the tools you need to bring it to an end if that is what you decide to do. This information is meant to empower you, not accuse you. This chapter may contradict what you believe to be true, so it's normal to experience some resistance, but my sincere hope is that you will engage with curiosity instead of judgment. Read the entire chapter with an open mind, then decide what you think about its contents.

If this chapter speaks to something you're currently experiencing, understand that you could not have been aware of its contents. Any benefits you derive from your pain are registered outside of your conscious awareness. It makes no sense to blame yourself for something you have been unaware of. Reading this information does not require anything of you; you are completely free to read it and reject it. However, I have been told by those who have embraced this information that it has forever altered the way they view the world—and this is true for me, as well.

It is not a welcome realization to learn that you have been using your pain to get what you want, but it can motivate you to change what you want or learn better behaviors to get it. What you choose to do with this information is up to you, but once you learn it, it is difficult to unlearn. If you feel resistant to the information, leave it. You can always revisit it later.

So far, we have focused on what we can directly control—our thoughts and our actions. This is the only chapter that delves into emotions and physiology because there is nothing you can do to directly change them. If you think you can try to tell someone who is depressed to simply cheer up or someone with a tension headache to just relax, it won't work!

Emotions and physiology are effective signals, and it is possible to indirectly change them by altering our thoughts and actions. This chapter explores how we use our emotions and physiology to control situations, and the people in our lives, to get what we want. Once you accept and examine this in your conscious awareness, you can decide if that is how you want to continue or if you would like to learn new solutions.

Choice Theory's Total Behavior

There is much research to support the notion that the mind and body are intricately connected, influencing each other. In Choice Theory, Glasser called this Total Behavior—the concept that all human behavior has four inseparable components: actions, thoughts, emotions, and our body's physiology. All components occur simultaneously in one behavior, the next behavior has its own set of components, and so on. There is never a behavior without all four components.

Glasser describes Total Behavior as a car with each behavioral component serving as a wheel. Actions and thoughts are the front wheels and emotions and physiology are the back wheels. When you drive a car, you can turn the front wheels to change the direction of the car, which indirectly causes the back wheels to follow—in other words, once you're aware of the painful feelings, you can redirect them by changing your thoughts and actions. Directly changing your actions and thoughts indirectly affects your emotions and physiology.

However, if your car is operating on autopilot—as when you subconsciously continue your pain to get the resulting benefits—you will never understand the need to change your actions or thoughts. Your emotions and physiology alert you with painful signals when life is not the way you want it to be, and if allowed to operate subconsciously, they direct the actions and thoughts that follow.

Once you understand that your subconscious creates those painful emotions and physiology to get something you want, you will likely want to change your actions and thoughts to positively affect those emotions and physiology. There are two functions of painful emotions and physiology—one serves you and the other may be something you will want to change.

Pain as a Signal

Stuck energy, in the form of unexpressed or unprocessed painful emotions, can literally kill you. This energy is experienced as stress in the body, and there is evidence of stress-induced medical problems like high blood pressure and heart disease. This stuck energy is not a stressor—external force does not create trapped energy in your body. It is what you think and do about those stressors that lead to the painful emotions that can become trapped in your body, causing pain and eventually illness.

Everyone has a virtual place—in their head, heart, or gut—that holds a vision of what their perfect world looks like. Choice Theory calls this the Quality World. While it can contain some traces of reality, the real world usually doesn't align with your Quality World. When things are in alignment, you feel generally satisfied and happy. When you're not getting what you think you want and deserve, painful emotions like sadness, anger, or anxiety occur. In these moments of evaluating or comparing what you want with what you're getting, you experience a brief flash of emotion, like a snap of your fingers, which tells you whether you have what you want or not. If you do, that brief signal is one of pleasure. If you do not, it is one of pain. You can't avoid that pain, even if you want to. You can stuff it down in the very next second, but this painful signal is raw, real, and authentic—and it happens fast. Its purpose is to help you make sense of your experience.

When you get what you want, the resulting emotion is an intrinsic reward—a sigh of contentment, a purring with pleasure. On the other hand, when you don't get what you want, that emotion can feel like a kick in the gut to let you know something is wrong and needs to be addressed. Your painful emotions, and sometimes physiology, are communicating to you that there is something requiring your attention. This is highly adaptive and works best when you notice it and tune in. Once you recognize something is wrong and figure out what that is, you're in a stronger position to do something about it.

You could save yourself so much misery by recognizing pain

as a signal to move on to problem-solving mode, but it's easy to ignore those early painful signals, allowing them to grow in size, duration, and intensity. These quick signals are typically experienced as frustration or satisfaction. When you experience satisfaction, you can work to maintain it or move on to another area that needs attention. Because the brain is hardwired for negativity, you can miss those moments of satisfaction as you remain focused on things you lack.

When you experience a painful frustration signal, pay attention, notice what is wrong, and do something about it. When you don't do something about it, you can end up like this:

> You're preparing for a trip, and as excited as you are, it comes with a full list of things that need to be done in addition to the regular routine of your life. There is packing, arranging for children and pets, getting ahead at work to compensate for your time away—the list goes on and on. During all the preparation, you get signals of exhaustion. Your body tells you to go to sleep but you push through, telling yourself, "I'm fine; I just got my second wind." On your trip, your body forces you to rest. You sleep through your plans because you chose to ignore the original signal.

It is like the light that comes on your car's dashboard when it's running out of fuel. You can ignore that light. Sometimes, you will successfully push it to the limit and still be able to refuel later. Other times, the car will sputter to a stop while you're driving. The ultimate goal is to fill up your tank before the light even comes on.

Your Mental Freedom thrives when you mindfully enjoy moments of satisfaction, peace, and happiness whenever they occur. Take the time to give thanks and express your gratitude. Our natural hardwiring for negativity makes it easy, often habitual, to seek out the next thing that is not the way you want it to be—even when nothing is wrong. This will rob you of Mental Freedom.

I can remember myself as a young mother when my two

sons, only 19 months apart in age, were always fighting. They were highly competitive with each other, and it often moved beyond yelling matches into physical fights, forcing me to intervene for safety's sake. On the rare occasions when they were not fighting, I would like to say that I noticed and felt gratitude for the peace in the house, but I did not. There was nothing requiring my immediate attention, so I spent that time searching through my mental to-do list for the next thing I could tackle. This may sound like a smart, expedient thing to do, but it was robbing me of my Mental Freedom.

When you find yourself looking for the next thing to do, ruminating on what the next painful situation could be, or anticipating the end of the good thing that is happening, use it as your signal to understand that there is nothing wrong at that moment. Take a deep breath, feel gratitude, and celebrate the wonderful moment. If you don't, those moments easily slip away as you keep yourself in stress mode.

Becoming an expert at noticing and attending to these early warning signals will greatly increase your Mental Freedom. Attend to the painful signals by fixing what is wrong and soak up the satisfying ones with mindfulness, gratitude, and celebration.

Pain as a Solution

When we avoid a problem, what starts as a painful signal has room to settle into becoming the solution.

While we are distracted by the excruciating pain, our subconscious recognizes the benefits of it. The pain clearly demonstrates to us that we are not getting what we want, but holding onto that pain indicates the presence of benefits that aren't so clear.

Think about the two examples mentioned. When you keep pushing to prepare for vacation, the benefit is that you will be able to relax knowing that you have adequately prepared for your absence and there is nothing to worry about. Maybe the decision to continue driving with the gas light on got you where you needed to be on time. Once you experience the benefit, the pain subconsciously becomes worth it.

Whether you consciously recognize the signal of frustration or not, your brain will work to find the solution. Strategizing with awareness, you get a say in what happens next. People don't generally plot and plan to experience pain, but operating on a subconscious level can result in doing things you would prefer not to do—as the information in this chapter will reveal.

For increased Mental Freedom, you want to address painful signals on a conscious level. Otherwise, you deprive yourself of response-ability. Practice acknowledging the pain you are experiencing and asking yourself, "What is this pain giving me? How is this pain my friend? What are the benefits I'm receiving from this pain?" Again, the pain I'm talking about is real. I'm not referring to people who are faking their pain, which is called malingering. While that serves its own purpose, it is not what I'm discussing in this chapter.

Painful emotions can be grouped into three general categories, each existing on a continuum. There is sadness, anger, and fear. Sadness can go from feeling down to feeling suicidal, anger can range from annoyed to furious, and fear can span from concern to pure terror. People can also experience painful physiology without medical origins. It feels like the pain just happens, and since there is nothing medically wrong, they believe there is nothing they can do about it.

Upon deep reflection, you may be able to see the benefits of the pain. When a benefit is realized, usually on a subconscious level, it can become a habit. Especially in a situation when nothing good is happening, you will maintain the pain for its benefits because that feels better than experiencing the pain without them. This allows the emotion or physiology to become an organized behavior, a habit, even after the initial problem has faded.

Ask yourself these questions: "What is it I want that I'm trying to get with this behavior? Is there something I can learn from this? Is this the behavior I want to use to get what I want?" Understand that emotions are purposeful; figure out what you are using this emotional or physical pain to obtain.

When my kids were growing up, Saturday would often be the day designated for housework, and my son, Kyle, was supposed to clean his room—but there were so many other things he preferred to do. Despite many prompts from me, he often did not do the one chore I expected of him. By the end of the day, I would be angry, yelling at him to clean his room. Someone who has not been exposed to these ideas might say that Kyle made me angry by not cleaning his room, and I would love to believe that; it lets me off the hook. But the truth is, after trying all my "nice mom" behaviors, I was finally bringing out the big guns. I was using my anger to intimidate him into doing what I wanted. He did not make me mad; I was using anger to get him to clean his room.

In movies, something you often hear therapist-type characters ask is, "How did that make you feel?" When you're on the path to Mental Freedom, you understand that examining your emotions lends very little to determining what you need to do in a situation. Your emotions exist as a signal, an experience that helps you understand if what is happening feels painful, pleasurable, or neutral.

As a counselor, I am only interested in feelings when my client is not sure how they interpret a situation. I might ask how they feel about it, but I would not ask that stereotypical counseling question, "How did that make you feel?" External forces cannot make anyone feel anything emotionally or physically. People choose to hold onto their pain to get an ounce of something pleasant—subconsciously at the cost of their own well-being and Mental Freedom.

It is equally untrue to say a person makes you happy, sad, mad, or anxious. No one has the power to make you feel anything. You choose your emotions, but without Mental Freedom techniques or some other empowering psychological processes, these choices don't happen consciously. Being aware of how you choose your emotions is true Mental Freedom.

This encompasses the concept that what happens to you is not as important as how you respond to it. You are powerless against the death of a loved one, the company you work for closing, or a natural disaster that destroys your home. There are endless possibilities for circumstances we have no control over to affect our lives, and you're not responsible for them. Our power and responsibility lie in how we choose to respond. Even in situations you did cause—like getting fired from your job not because the company is closing but because of poor performance—you always have the ability to choose how you respond. And if you are not getting what you want, it is your responsibility to fix it.

You relinquish your power to address things beyond your control when you assign the responsibility for not getting what you want to other people. For example, you asked your partner to make dinner for the kids because you wanted to visit with friends, but your partner forgot, causing you to cancel your plans. You might decide the thing to do is blame your spouse and give them the silent treatment, but by placing your partner at the center of the problem, you indirectly make them responsible for fixing it. Instead of going into problem-solving mode, you allow the frustration to linger to punish your partner for messing up your plans. The anger is no longer helping you; it is working against you.

When you choose to hold onto that anger, it ceases being a signal and becomes a behavior you use to communicate how important your plans were, and maybe that your partner better make it up to you. Consciously, you believe your spouse made you mad. This is simply not true. You are choosing anger because you believe it's the best way to get what you want, which might be an apology and some kind of restitution.

It is possible this strategy could work, but it is also a good example of using your emotions against yourself. Every time you do this, you damage your relationships. Believing it is not only your right but also your responsibility to control loved ones with anger, sadness, fear, or disgust—even when you believe it is for their own good—you engage in behaviors that are destructive to your most important relationships.

Decide who you want to be in any given situation and act in congruence with who that person is. You are never at the mercy of your emotions. You can switch from annoyance to understanding by reminding yourself that your partner could have had something pressing that caused them to forget your plans. You can take responsibility for not sending a reminder. Going into problem-solving mode, you could decide to take advantage of a cozy evening at home or choose to meet up with your friends later. This way, even when you are not necessarily responsible for the original situation, you are choosing to be response-able.

When you find it difficult to shift your pain to something better, ask yourself, "What do I want that this pain provides me?" The behavior is always adaptive and purposeful, but it is not always responsible, meaning you get something you want at the expense of others getting what they want. I have the control to shift from feeling frustration to understanding just by changing my thoughts—and with some practice, you can, too.

Purposes of Pain

In Choice Theory psychology, Glasser taught that all behavior is purposeful, designed to get what we want. Listed below are some benefits I have heard clients discover they receive from their physical and emotional pain:

1. People notice when you're in pain and give you attention, often providing help without you needing to ask for it. This is particularly beneficial for people with a high Freedom need and subsequent strong independence streak.

2. Less is expected of you when you're sad, angry, or anxious, allowing you to avoid your responsibilities.

3. Anxiety can protect you. If you're afraid, you will not try things that could hurt you. You can stay safe.

4. Depressing can help slow life down, giving you time to contemplate your next steps.

5. Denying or ignoring your emotions creates internal pressure from holding them in. Having a good cry or exploding with a temper tantrum can release all the built-up energy from your emotions and make you feel good in the moment. The flipside of a temper tantrum, however, often comes with collateral damage.

6. Depressing can demonstrate to others how broken you are when you suffer a loss, and consequently, how important that loss was to you.

7. While grieving, you keep the person you have lost active in your perception. The alternative is that they are just gone, so it is preferable to stay in the grief.

8. Anger can be used to pump you up when you feel small and insignificant.

9. Anger and depression can be used as punishment for a perceived wrong when directed toward a specific individual.

10. Your pain can be used to control others when you blame them for your pain, thus placing responsibility on them to fix it. Your pain can also be used to control others by guilting them into spending time with you, treating you with compassion, or taking care of tasks that are your responsibility.

11. Depressing can keep you safe. For example, if you are having any suicidal or homicidal thoughts, depressing will take away your energy and clarity of thought so you will be unable to formulate plans, let alone follow through on them.

12. On a more positive note, anger can lead to social change. History is full of evidence that anger and violence are essential for societal change, as the oppressed are systematically left with no other options.

13. Once you have used a behavior and received a benefit, it can become a habit. Even when it no longer

works to your benefit, the habit can remain without psychological intervention. Most of us can relate to having a whiny person in our life. In the beginning, you try to help. However, by offering them your attention, they learn that their complaining has benefits, so they continue. It is not easy to keep trying to help when they meet every suggestion with a "yeah, but," so you stop participating. Even though their behavior is no longer supplying the benefit of attention they got in the beginning, they don't stop because there was a time when it worked, and subconsciously, they are counting on it working again.

If these reasons don't resonate with you because you only allow yourself to experience pain when you are alone, consider that when you hide your pain from others, it is because you're trying to control yourself.

It is also possible that you're using your behavior to release some pent-up energy, as described in No. 5. Using painful emotions when you're alone often translates to an attempt to force yourself into doing something that you really do not want to do or are scared to do. Privately holding onto sadness, shame, or guilt is a way to punish yourself before anyone else can.

I once worked with a counselor who developed a bad case of laryngitis. Her doctor put her on antibiotics and thought that would solve the problem, but even after several rounds of medication, she continued to have no voice. Finally, her doctor warned her that she may never recover her voice; laryngitis can be permanent. As someone who made a living using her voice, she was terrified, but she surrendered to the situation because there seemed to be nothing left to try. Not only was the woman a counselor but she was also a trainer of Choice Theory. While rereading William Glasser's book, she came across his concepts about the aches and pains most people accept as part of everyday living and the aging process. She thought about her laryngitis—could it be a physical manifestation of an issue she was avoiding?

This reflection revealed that she had no voice in her

relationship, and upon acknowledging this, she discovered the relationship was no longer working for her. The next morning, she woke up to the phone ringing, picked it up, and said, "Hello." For the first time in six months, she had a voice.

It's likely my colleague was using her pain to motivate herself to end a relationship that had become toxic. She has not looked back and believes she will never have that type of laryngitis again. I tend to agree.

The Question of Mental Illness

Mental Freedom and Choice Theory psychology offer alternative perspectives regarding the etiology of mental distress that are strength-based and person-centered, unlike psychiatric and pharmaceutical companies that are based on a disease model of mental health problems, disorders, or illnesses. There is an incredible amount of material that can help you understand how mental disorders are the mind's way of responding to and compensating for the experiences and circumstances in one's life. As a counselor who practices by this concept, any symptoms I see in a client that might lead me to a Diagnostic and Statistical Manual diagnosis are theorized as compensatory behaviors to events, often trauma, in their lives, not chemical imbalances or diseases that just happen to people. They are purposeful and serve the person in the situation they are in. It is too much for me to go into here, so I suggest that you investigate for yourself and decide what you believe.

(If you would like to investigate these ideas further, here are my recommendations: *Depression Delusion* by Dr. Terry Lynch, *Anatomy of an Epidemic* by Robert Whitaker, *Your Drug May Be Your Problem* by Dr. Peter Breggin, *The Myth of Mental Illness* by Thomas Szasz, *Deadly Medicines and Organised Crime* by Pete Gøotzche, and *Warning: Psychiatry May be Hazardous to Your Mental Health* by William Glasser.)

Anyone with a mental health condition has found behaviors

that provide them with a modicum of something they want. Sometimes, that behavior is the best they have in the situation to help themselves. Other times, they may be ready to learn more adaptable, less disruptive ways of coping. The decision is completely theirs.

Dissociative identity disorder, formerly known as multiple personality disorder, effectively illustrates this point. This diagnosis often involves a history of horrific, ritualistic, and frequent sexual abuse by a member of their own household—someone who should have been protecting them. This incredibly painful treatment led them to develop the amazing, protective skill of dissociation. If someone I loved was in a similar situation, I would hope and pray that they could develop that skill.

Once that effective behavior is developed, it becomes a go-to behavior anytime the person experiences anxiety. They have created a well-traveled neural pathway that links dissociation with anxiety. However, once the person is away from the abuse, they might find living a life with frequent dissociative episodes becomes dysfunctional and seek treatment. But it is not a disorder, a disease, or a character flaw—it is a superpower! If this person came to me for help, I would view their continued use of disassociation as a habit, not a mental disorder. It was a highly adaptive behavior that is no longer needed in the same way it once was, but it helped the person survive something no human should endure.

If you want to develop better behaviors to address your painful emotions and physiology, understand that you are not required to first give up the behavior you want to change. In fact, progress will happen faster if you focus on developing new behaviors rather than giving up the ones that no longer serve you. But by understanding the subconscious benefits of holding onto pain, you no longer need to be at the mercy of those behaviors. Shift those benefits into your awareness by acknowledging pain as a signal to self-evaluate and determine what the pain is doing for you. Then, you can choose whether you want to continue the behavior or not. If you decide you want to find other ways to achieve those benefits, you can work to develop them by being true to the person you want to be. Glasser said, "It is almost impossible for anyone, even the most ineffective among us, to continue to choose misery after becoming aware that it is a choice."

Unconditional Trust for Self

If you have been using your pain to control other people, remember that it has been happening without your knowledge. Now that you are aware, feeling guilt and shame about it is normal, but it is misplaced. It doesn't make sense to create guilt and shame around a behavior you did not know you were doing. In this situation, you're using guilt and shame to communicate to yourself and others that you regret what you have been doing and plan to do better in the future. Do not punish yourself for whatever you have done in the past. Instead, practice the Unconditional Trust Challenge with yourself by understanding that you were doing the best you could. Engage nonjudgment, compassion, and forgiveness for yourself. Why judge yourself for doing your best with the information available to you at that time?

Emotions and physical pain are authentic. You are experiencing real pain, but you're also communicating to others that they need to change so you can be happy. If someone else is trying to control you with their emotions or physiology, you need to decide what you want out of that situation. Will you supply what they want, try to negotiate a win/win solution, or refuse to comply?

Do not kill the messenger—your pain is not the problem. It has been your friend in the past, helping you get what you want. You may want something different now, or you may want to learn a better way to get it, but don't hate yourself or your pain. You were using the best behavior you had at the time to get the most of what you wanted. Your pain is the messenger, not the creator—that role belongs to your subconscious. Once your motivation is conscious, you get to decide how you want to respond.

Respond, Do Not React

There is an important distinction between reacting and responding: You react when you allow external forces to generate a quick, knee-jerk behavior without thinking about what is best. A response requires reflection to inform your next choice. This quote, often attributed to Viktor Frankl, illustrates this: "Between stimulus and response, there is a space. In that space lies our freedom and power to choose our response. In our response lies our growth and freedom." Developing Mental Freedom for yourself allows you to expand that space.

People may accuse you of using your pain to control others, but just because this is their observation does not mean it is the truth. Practice objectively examining feedback from others without allowing yourself to be defensive. The people in your life can illuminate your blind spots, but you must first decide for yourself if there is truth in what they see and whether you want to change.

One day, when talking with my son, Kyle, about one of his friends being grounded again, I said, "His mom is such a control freak." Kyle responded, "Mom, you're the most controlling person I know. You are so nice to people that they can't say no to you." I was taken aback by this accusation as I was actively working to remove controlling behaviors from my repertoire. After some self-evaluation, I realized Kyle's observation was not my truth. Yes, I was nice to people, but my motivation was to match the person I want to be: a kind and loving person. Kyle's perception was more about him wanting to push back against my parental authority—something he found hard to do because I was kind and supportive.

Pay attention when others share their opinions about you and your behavior, especially if they are someone whose opinions you value and respect. You may be experiencing a blind spot that someone close to you can illuminate. This can be challenging when they bring up something that contradicts your perception of yourself, but it is beneficial to spend the time assessing if there is accuracy in what they see. If you don't see it, engage your curiosity to explore the observations, but remember that you are the ultimate authority on yourself and your behavior. If you have worked to understand their analysis and decided it doesn't fit your narrative of who you are, simply let it go. If you find it does have accuracy, then decide what you want to do about it.

THE FLIP SIDE

Not only does this information provide you with tools to address how you use your pain; it also allows you to recognize when others are using their pain to control you. It's possible that this chapter has allowed you to recognize times when you allowed yourself to be controlled by someone else's pain. Remain compassionate because it is unlikely that they consciously chose to do so.

If this information resonates with you, you will see these situations differently. Even though it is difficult to see someone in pain, you will no longer believe you must respond as if you have no choice. Recognize that you are not responsible for someone else's pain, remember the difference between responsibility and response-ability, and apply the Unconditional Trust Challenge by remembering their behavior is not being done with malice toward you; it is simply the best way the person in pain knows how to get what they want.

You get to decide exactly how you will respond. You can continue to help with the understanding that you do not have to help because of guilt; you want to help because you are concerned. You can set boundaries about when and how you will help. You might buy them a copy of this book and see if they can recognize themselves in this chapter, and you can support them through that. It is also your right to decide to stop helping altogether. An option I don't recommend, you can choose resentment and frustration as your best attempts to get them to stop controlling you, thus repeating the cycle. Whatever you choose to do is now your responsibility. See how that works?

Options for Coping with Your Pain

There are three ways to cope with your pain. One way of coping is to wallow in the emotion. People might do this as a way to understand the painful feeling, but the only benefit of understanding your pain is in that brief moment when it signals that you are not getting what you want. Unless you are trying to figure out what the pain might be doing for you, there is no tangible benefit to studying your emotions. Another way to cope is to deny or ignore your pain—a dangerous method, as it can lead to physical problems. Avoiding your pain for a prolonged period, whether by stuffing it away or pretending everything is fine, can cause the emotion to erupt like an old-time pressure cooker or manifest as an illness. The third option is to transform the emotion, a concept that will be introduced in the next chapter.

Approach your pain with curiosity by asking yourself, "What do I want that I'm trying to get through my sadness/anger/anxiety/pain?" When you figure out what that is and decide to address it, you can work at getting what you want in more responsible ways.

You are responsible for your own happiness. When you're not getting what you want, take the steps to fix it:

- You have every right to ask for what you want but know it is a request, not a demand. Do not expect others to prioritize what you want over what they want. They might comply; they might not. Do not get mad, sad, or anxious if they do not. Just chalk it up to the fact that people do the best they know to get what they want in every situation—and they have every right to do that, just like you.

- You could change your behavior and try something different. Instead of emotionally extorting people, you could do something that could result in them choosing to do what you want because it corresponds to something they want.

- You could change or adjust what you want.
- You could change your perception of the situation by rewriting the stories in your head about what is happening.

In these ways, you are transforming your painful emotions into satisfying emotions. Should the pain persist, you can consider the following:

1. You are still receiving a benefit from the pain. Remove yourself from the immediate situation and examine what holding onto your pain could be doing for you with curiosity so you can gain conscious control.
2. You have used this behavior for so long that it has become a habit.
3. You are having difficulty applying this information to your life. There are Mental Freedom group coaching sessions that can help you, which will be discussed in chapter nine, "The Head, Heart, and Hands."

Summary:

1. Our pain exists for two purposes: to alert us that something is wrong and to get us something we want.
2. When something is happening that doesn't match the way we want things to be, the painful signal is designed to motivate us to do something about it.
3. Ignoring the signal can create bigger problems for us, so it is best to act quickly.
4. When we fail to act quickly, the subconscious discovers the benefits that come with the pain, allowing the pain to persist—even though it may be excruciating.
5. Once those benefits register subconsciously, the pain becomes our solution: the best way we know how to gain even a modicum of pleasure in an otherwise incredibly painful situation.

6. Combine this lesson with the Unconditional Trust Challenge to foster compassion for ourselves and others who may have used emotional extortion and physical pain to control people and situations around them. It was not done consciously, and they were doing the best they knew at the time to get a little of what they wanted, as were you.

7. Once we can decipher the benefit we receive, we can consciously develop alternative behaviors that are not manipulative to achieve the same benefits.

Appreciating the GLOW

"Every negative situation contains the possibility for something positive, an opportunity. It is how you look at it that matters." –Robert Greene

The GLOW can transform your life in ways you did not believe were possible. It unlocks a different path through painful events—everything from disappointing day-to-day incidents to extreme life-altering circumstances like loss or trauma. How do I know? Because this is the very process I used when I was still reeling from the death of my 37-year-old husband.

The reason I wrote this book is to provide people with the tools they need to build their own Mental Freedom. This chapter presents concepts you must be ready, willing, and able to accept. You may not be ready, and that is okay; this book has no expiration date. When you do feel ready and willing to appreciate the GLOW, this chapter will provide you with the tools to make you able. Your journey will unfold on your own timeline, and the GLOW will be there when you are ready to embrace it. This knowledge provides a shortcut that bypasses the time needed to reveal hindsight, offering balance as soon as you are ready: Whenever you encounter a painful situation, you can remember there is not only pain—there is also an equal amount of positivity. If you strongly resist this idea, please read on with curiosity and ask yourself the question, "What if this information really is the truth?"

I attended a workshop a few months after my husband, Dave, died in 1999. One of the presenters introduced me to John Demartini's idea that all events in our lives are balanced with an equal amount of positivity and negativity. It wasn't until three years after my husband's death that Demartini published his book, *The Breakthrough Experience*, to flesh out those ideas, but fortunately, the information found me right when I needed it.

Remember the periodic table? It describes the known elements of the universe, and each has a positive and negative charge that is perfectly balanced with the same number of protons and electrons. From that fact, Demartini extrapolated the idea that our life events are the same—equally balanced.

Because of our negativity bias, we are quick to notice the negative side without ever considering the positive. The intense experience of unwanted change as shock, pain, or grief can cloud any view beyond the negative for some time. This scientific fact of balance means that the reverse is true: Choices we have been socialized to believe are inherently positive—such as getting married, having children, earning a promotion, or attending college—also come with huge trade-offs, which can create painful situations that we couldn't let ourselves see through the cloud of unbalanced positivity. While this is true, it is not relevant to appreciating the GLOW. There is no benefit in seeking out the negatives that come with the positive circumstances of your life, but it's important to understand that the balance is always there.

My husband's illness from chronic myelogenous leukemia, and subsequent death, was the most painful experience of my life. Rating it on a scale from one to 100, with one being an iota of discomfort and 100 being the worst pain imaginable, I gave it an 87. Considering the balance in all things, if there is 87 in negativity, there must also be 87 in positivity. This was too hard for me to grasp during that workshop so soon after his death, but a few months later, I began to explore the concepts.

It seemed wrong to consider the idea that positivity could be associated with my husband's death, but my teenage sons were going through their own experiences with grief. My desire to help them got me pondering the horrible question: *What could be good about my husband's death?* It sounded sick. How could I ask a question like that? Yet, I came up with two answers once I remembered my boys.

The first positive result of Dave's death I discovered was the opportunity to say goodbye. Our relationships with him were all in order. The last words we spoke were not spoken in anger, nor were they inconsequential. This is not an opportunity everyone gets, and it's one that many wish for when it's too late.

The second was all the time he could spend with his family after leaving his job—not because he was too sick to work, but because he did not want to further expose himself to the probable cause of his illness. The chemical benzene was linked to his type of leukemia, and it was something he came into regular contact with as a mechanic. He spent his newfound free time with our boys, coaching both their Little League and soccer teams, taking them to all their wrestling tournaments, and teaching them mechanics and carpentry. We even had the chance to take a special vacation to Disney World. Since my husband was quite a workaholic, this would not have happened had he been healthy and lived to be 100. It was truly a gift.

This was not enough to balance the scales, but it gave me a glimpse into what was possible, and time revealed the rest:

- In 1998, my friends, my husband, and I raised enough money to add 350 people to the bone marrow registry. None of them matched my husband, but some went on to donate life-saving bone marrow to others. People were saved because Dave's illness called his community to support this cause.

- His best friend was able to come out as a gay man, something he would not do while my husband was alive. Dave had harsh, misguided beliefs, and his friend decided it was better to keep his truth to himself rather than deal with the potential fallout.

- Dave's experience with that chemical, benzene, shed light on the risks, and more mechanics wear latex gloves when they work on engines.

- And finally, there's my life's work. I started to travel the world in 2001, wrote my first book in 2006 and four more since, and became the Director of William

Glasser International in 2013. My work led me to help others through their pain, and now, I'm presenting the culmination of it all to you in this book. If my husband were still alive, I would still be living in Pennsylvania, working at the foster care agency I left to start my own business in Chicago.

My mother-in-law would never have wanted to search for positivity resulting from Dave's death. She used her grief to show the world how much she loved him by suffering the rest of her life, and she believed moving on would mean she wasn't the kind of mother she wanted to be. Although I wish she could have used this information to alleviate some of her pain, some people don't want to leave it behind. All we can do is present the information.

Around the time I had begun developing the concept of GLOW, I had the chance to present it in a group therapy session at a drug and alcohol rehab center. I asked the group of women to find anything positive resulting from the worst thing that had ever happened to them they'd be willing to share using the categories of gifts, lessons, opportunities, and wisdom to frame their search.

Taking turns around the circle, it was clear they really understood the exercise. There were many great examples, but one woman's response stands out in my memory. At first, she angrily cried, "I found my father hanging from the end of a rope! What could be good about that?" Her venomous declaration took me aback, but I told her that only she could know the answer and to think about it some more. After everyone else contributed their answers, I went back to her to find tears rolling down her cheeks. I asked what she had figured out, and she said, "If my father had not died, my sister and I would be living in the streets. It was his life insurance that allowed us to buy a house for ourselves." It was a powerful first step toward appreciating the GLOW.

Another example that comes to mind is from a young teacher who had recently graduated with a degree in education. As a student teacher, she was paired with a terribly mean elementary school teacher who was horrible to her students. She reported,

"It is as if she hates them. What could be good about that?" Once again, I did not have the answer, but I asked what kind of relationship she formed with the students. "I had great relationships with my students," she said. I had suspected as much, so I asked if she would have fostered such great relationships if they already had strong connections with their teacher. She was quiet for a moment before admitting, "No, probably not." It was just a guess on my part, but I had found one aspect of GLOW in that painful situation. Naturally, there will be more than that, but it was a beginning to start her on her path to balance.

Appreciating the GLOW does not mean that you would not give it all up if you could. That student teacher likely would have chosen a nicer teacher if given the chance. If I could rewind the clock and have my husband back, I would, and I'm sure that woman who was able to recognize a benefit of her father's death would too. But we don't get to choose our tragedies; all we get to do is find a way to live with them and push forward. If you can train yourself to find the GLOW, you will not need hindsight to soften your pain. It has become my immediate reaction to unwanted circumstances. When I broke both of my ankles in a hot air balloon accident in 2014, I said to myself, "Well, Kim, now you have the *opportunity* to practice what you preach." This is something that develops with practice. When it feels difficult, don't be discouraged, but push through and keep trying. The more you do, the quicker you'll find the path out of misery when you want one.

Imagine coming across a dirty old coin. You can just barely make out the front, so you polish it to reveal the details before putting it in your pocket. There could be many reasons why you didn't think to flip that coin over and look at the back, but you took it as is and decided to carry it with you. When you get around to turning the coin over, you'll discover it is much filthier than the front. You could leave it as is, but if you are committed to viewing both sides, you will start scrubbing. It will take more time and energy than the side that first faced up at you, but soon, you can begin to discern what is there.

Pain can feel all-consuming, but the passing of time makes it easy to appreciate all the ways you wouldn't be who you are today without that experience. This information is designed to help you shorten that process. When you experience pain, you can trust that there is positivity equal to the pain involved. You may not be ready to look for it yet but take comfort in the fact that it is there for you to find.

WHAT EXACTLY IS THE GLOW?

Appreciating the GLOW is a mindset that facilitates mental adaptability during and after challenging experiences. I created the GLOW acronym to represent the different ways positivity reveals itself through pain: gifts, lessons, opportunities, and wisdom. The brain's hardwiring for negativity directs our focus to the difficulty, fear, sadness, and struggle rather than the GLOW, but the GLOW is always present.

> **Gifts** that can be accepted
>
> **Lessons** that can be learned
>
> **Opportunities** that can be taken advantage of to benefit yourself or others
>
> **Wisdom** that flourished from putting your lessons into practice

The idea that there is a positive side to painful situations may hold no truth for you right now. Perhaps you cannot begin to appreciate the GLOW because you believe it means you were not truly invested. If I can appreciate the GLOW resulting from my husband's death, does that mean I didn't love him deeply enough? This idea of holding onto grief to prove something harkens back to those stories we fabricate and maintain in our heads, discussed in chapter six, "Rewriting the Stories in Your Head." If this relates to why you're holding onto pain, recognize that it is a story you made up and determine if it is helping or hindering your Mental Freedom.

The GLOW does not negate the pain you have experienced.

That pain is real, and it can be excruciating, but its existence implies an equal amount of GLOW. Learning to find and appreciate the GLOW can neutralize that pain. This process doesn't take the pain away, but it balances the scales so the pain no longer weighs you down. This reframes your situation, taking you from the experience of pain to the journey of finding the benefits of your challenges.

Appreciating the GLOW does not mean you would decline a ride in a time machine to a less painful time, but we don't get to rewind the clock. All we can do is the best we can to make sense of our pain and find a way to move forward. The pain will still be there, but once you find an equal amount of GLOW to neutralize it, you are much freer to engage with happiness.

The great news is that, no matter what you have been through in life, you are not broken. You don't have to always feel the way you do now. Things can get better.

There is no expectation that you will be able to find an equal amount of GLOW to balance the pain in one sitting. It would be almost impossible to do that, particularly considering the high number of some of the pain you may have experienced. The sole fact that you lived through a painful experience gives you an opportunity to illuminate the way for others in a similar situation. Just because the opportunity exists doesn't make it an obligation, but it is an opportunity, nonetheless. The hope is that you can find at least one thing; finding that one thing is evidence that the GLOW exists. Once you know what you are looking for, you can open yourself to the possibility of finding more.

The categories of gifts, lessons, opportunities, and wisdom exist to stimulate your thinking and help you in your search, not to represent strict guidelines. Simply use the categories as areas to mine for possibilities. You may occasionally find there are no precious finds in some of the categories.

You are free to decide that certain painful times of your life are off-limits when it comes to searching for the GLOW. It is always your choice what, if anything, you do with this information. However, understand that mining for the GLOW is a process;

it's not designed to happen all at once. It has helped many of my clients navigate their grief, and they report experiencing life-transforming benefits.

SHIFTING FOCUS

Sometimes the GLOW becomes visible with a simple flip of that coin, shifting focus from the negative to the positive.

After that hot air balloon accident, lying in bed with two broken ankles, I began feeling sorry for myself. Shifting gears to the GLOW, I remembered when my friend broke both her elbows and had them in hard casts, bent and positioned in front of her about chest high. She was unable to feed herself, blow her nose, or wipe her own butt. Remembering her situation filled me with gratitude that the only thing I could not do was walk. At least I could still feed myself, blow my nose, and wipe my own butt. It would have been easy to focus on what I couldn't do, as people naturally tend to do. But armed with this knowledge, it was just as easy to shift to gratitude for everything I could do.

Similarly, you might be focusing on the things you want that you do not have. You can strive for that college diploma, happily-ever-after relationship, or promotion at work, but while you do, remember to be grateful for what you already have.

When you're focused on something important you have lost, I have always found this quote by Dr. Seuss helpful: "Don't cry because it's over; smile because it happened." Let yourself cry if you need to, but when you are finished, remember to smile because you had an amazing person or opportunity in your life, even if it did not last as long as you would have liked. The experience of having someone so important to you that it is painful without them is a gift in itself—an aspect of GLOW that helped me through my grief when my husband died. Some people never encounter that level of love and care.

Focusing on what we do not have happens when you compare yourself to others. It is more fruitful to compare your current self to a past version of yourself instead. "Am I better today than

I was yesterday?" is a much better question than, "Am I better than them?"

Once you begin collecting the GLOW from your painful situations, it will help you accept what has happened. Fighting against the reality of your life will never lead you toward increased Mental Freedom. Instead, it brings its own degree of misery. Scott D'Alterio, a Choice Theory instructor and friend of mine, puts it plainly: "Your pain is proportional to your resistance."

The way you deal with painful situations will create neural pathways connecting you to behaviors you can use again. If you have been engaged with your default wiring for negativity, the brain will continue to lead you down the path of least resistance to the same emotions and behaviors. (As neuropsychologist Donald Hebb said, "Neurons that fire together, wire together.") The GLOW offers an alternative track, guiding you to positively disrupt the negative neural connection by consciously choosing something different.

In 2021, I adopted a mantra that helped me reframe my thinking: "Nothing happens *to* me; everything happens *for* me." The challenge is to remember these words in the initial moment of resistance and frustration. And once you can accept each moment as it comes, gratitude is not much further.

The GLOW is always there within the pain; you just need to be willing to find it. Appreciating the GLOW is a gift of Mental Freedom that will keep on giving for the rest of your life.

Summary

1. Each event in your life is equally balanced with positive and negative outcomes, without exception.
2. The timing for appreciating the GLOW is critical and should never be rushed. The person experiencing the pain gets to decide when they are ready to look for it.
3. When searching for the positives in your painful experiences, the acronym GLOW—gifts, lessons,

opportunities, and wisdom—can help narrow your search.

4. There are people who will resist finding the GLOW for their own personal reasons, and this is fine. It is not something to push on someone.

5. Shift your focus from what you can't do and what you do not have to what you can do and what you do have.

6. Fighting the reality of your life robs you of Mental Freedom. You can't change the things that have already happened; accept your circumstances and move forward.

7. Once you reach acceptance, it becomes easier to find gratitude in what already exists while striving for more, if more is what you want.

The Head, Heart, and Hands of Mental Freedom

At the end of this chapter, you will have completed the first step of your Mental Freedom journey—the head component to the head, heart, and hands of Mental Freedom. The understanding of what Mental Freedom is and the principles it espouses needs to be in place before you can move on to the heart area of your journey.

Wanting to share what you read in a self-help book is understandable, but without applying what you've learned to your life, the information is hollow. It is only through the heart piece of Mental Freedom, your personal implementation of the material the head piece provides, that you can offer your first-hand experiences to others in a more meaningful and effective way.

After the heart journey, if you choose to be response-able for helping others, you can start sharing the head and heart parts of your Mental Freedom journey with others who ask for your help. This is what I call the hands part of your journey. Even if you are already a counselor, social worker, psychologist, or coach, I hope you will achieve the heart piece before embarking on the hands portion of your journey. (In my certification program, I only invite people to become trainers who have shared their Mental Freedom heart journey with my team. Without that in place, their teaching will fall flat.)

It's so easy to read a book, move on to the next one, and eventually forget most of what you read. I hope you decide to not let that happen with *Mental Freedom: You Hold the Key*. Depending on your time and budget, there are many steps you can take beyond reading this book if you choose to do so.

Do It Yourself

If you feel confident in your ability to navigate on your own with the tools you gained from this book, then congratulations. I recommend downloading the Mental Freedom PDF workbook (olverinternational.com/product/mental-freedom-workbook) to help hold you accountable as you navigate toward your own deeply felt sense of Mental Freedom.

If you want some assistance with applying Mental Freedom to a specific situation, coaching or counseling can help. We have a directory of counselors and coaches ready to help you virtually at olverinternational.com/directory.

The in-person Mental Freedom Experience consists of six sessions that delve into each of the Mental Freedom principles. Available as both an individual or group program, the Mental Freedom Experience begins with the complimentary, prerecorded Mental Freedom Masterclass found at courses.olverinternational.com/masterclass-signup.

Unlike typical counseling, the in-person Mental Freedom Experience program doesn't require people to share their problems with their practitioners. Of course, they can share if they want to, but practitioners do not need that information to be able to help at their fullest capacity. It's not that those things aren't important, but talking about them often just creates more misery. The Mental Freedom Experience doesn't take months or years as conventional counseling or therapy sessions do; it only takes six sessions. And if you want to go beyond those first six sessions to help solidify those concepts, have some accountability, and a personalized solution for your specific situation, then you can do that.

Certification

If you are a human services professional who would like to become certified in Mental Freedom, you will begin with the Mental Freedom Masterclass mentioned above.

After completing your Mental Freedom Experience, you will receive the Mental Freedom Curriculum—six more sessions that guide you through an in-depth exploration into how to present the Mental Freedom Experience to your clients, both in counseling and coaching. Finally, you will conduct the Mental Freedom Experience with your own clients, either individually or in groups. As you do that, you will also receive seven supervision sessions with me or a member of my team before you are awarded your Mental Freedom certification.

Trainer

Mental Freedom trainers certify others in Mental Freedom. This level of accomplishment is by invitation only, extended to those who have undergone meaningful transformation through their Mental Freedom Experience who I believe would make great trainers of the model. Those invited and interested will be interviewed by myself and two other members of my team. If the vote is unanimous, you can become one of our trainers. The process involves watching me facilitate a Mental Freedom Experience, followed by us facilitating one together, before someone from the team watches you facilitate one on your own. When the decision is unanimous again, you will become a trainer.

Conclusion

The path to complete Mental Freedom is paved by implementing all the principles designed to Open Your Heart, Free Your Mind, and Transform Your Life. However, you are completely in charge of your journey and do not have to apply everything you've just learned. If you find sacrificing some of your Mental Freedom in some situations is the best choice, you always have that option. You are in control. Even if you only implement one of the suggestions in this book, you will increase your Mental Freedom. The more you do, the freer you will become. Naturally, I want to see you grow to become as free as you can possibly be, but I also respect the pace you set for yourself and your ability to prioritize something above your own Mental Freedom.

Everything you have learned in the chapters in this book is yours for the rest of your life. Whenever you are struggling to hold onto your Mental Freedom, ask yourself, "Which of these lessons do I need to practice most in this moment?" There will always be an answer. If you can't find it on your own, schedule a couple of Mental Freedom sessions with one of our practitioners and specialists.

Should you have any questions or want some help, visit the Mental Freedom community on Facebook or contact info@olverinternational.com.

Acknowledgments

This is a part of the book I am excited to write to express gratitude for all those who have helped me on this journey of writing *Mental Freedom: You Hold the Key*. I also have some fear that I may leave out someone important. If you know you belong here and I didn't mention you, please know it wasn't intentional.

I want to start with gratitude to my lifetime mentor, William Glasser, M.D., the psychiatrist who started my entire adult career and life with his principles of Choice Theory® psychology. I learned these concepts in 1987, forming the foundation of everything I do, including this book. Choice Theory is the foundation upon which Mental Freedom is built. Beyond Dr. Glasser, there were several Choice Theory friends and colleagues who helped me think through these principles: Patricia Robey, EdD; Sylvester Baugh, CTRTC; Scott D'Alterio, EdD; and Barnes Boffey.

I want to thank the Universe for bringing Nikki Burnett into my life. She is a young woman I met when I was in Australia for a speaking engagement in 2019. There was just something about her I really liked. I was concerned when I saw she was going through a tough time on Facebook, so I reached out to her to see if she would be willing to allow me to teach her the raw, untested, preliminary Mental Freedom process. She said yes and became the OG of Mental Freedom. I will forever be grateful to her for trusting me to share these ideas with her.

I also need to express gratitude for the pandemic that provided the opportunity to slow my life down enough to reflect on the concepts that would eventually become this book.

The following people helped me with specific pieces of this book: Dr. Scott D'Alterio for the prison visual as the opposite of Mental Freedom; Vince Thompson for inspiring the "Unconditional Trust Challenge;" Kathy Hatton for breaking her elbows, which helped me practice the GLOW when I broke my ankles; Byron Waller, PhD, LCPC, for helping me see the inherent racism in one of the stories I shared and assisting me to rework that story to reflect its true meaning; Sue Berry, BSc, Grad Dip T for helping me realize the brain can create not just emotional but also physical pain without biological causes; Michael Fulkerson, MAE, LPCC-S who showed me a less combative way to compare Mental Freedom with the current medical model; Anasuya Jegathevi Jegathesan, PhD, who assisted me with seeing the American ethnocentrism I had unconsciously written with; Ken Pierce, psychologist, who taught me John Demartini's concept of balance in all our life experiences; Marci Shimoff and Mary Allen, MCC for providing quotes for the cover of this book; and Teresa Greco, OCT, MEd, for writing the foreword to this book.

I'd also like to acknowledge those who gave me the opportunity to present my initial Mental Freedom concepts in person: Shana O'Boyle, MS, CTRTC, and Steve Hammond, MEd the first people who allowed me to present Mental Freedom at their staff retreat in August 2021; Dubravka Stijačić, PRT, ECP, for giving me the opportunity to present Mental Freedom abroad for the first time in March 2023; and Dr. Patricia Robey for allowing me to teach Mental Freedom to one of her undergraduate classes in June 2023. I am also grateful to Cindi Coffman, BA, CADC, CCS who allowed me to teach Mental Freedom to four of her counselors at St. Joshep's Rehabilitation Center.

I am also so grateful to those who were instrumental in my efforts to do some research for these ideas. First was Nasrollah Navid, MD for suggesting I do the research in the first place. Second was Cameron B. Richardson, PhD, a friend and researcher from Penn State, who helped me design the research. After that, I recruited a group of counselors and coaches to earn their Mental Freedom certification so they could present Mental Freedom to the experimental groups for the research project. Those Mental Freedom pioneers were Sylvester Baugh; Emily C. Benjamin, CAADC; Farida Dsilva Dias, MBA, MA, PhD; Christine Duffield, MEd; Aleksandra Dzięciołowska-Piatek; Maryam Yama Gidado, CW2, USAR; Teresa Greco, OCT, MEd; Zahra Khoshnevisan, PhD; Sue Kranz, CTRTC; Grant Rusty Long, CASC; Vasuki Mathivanan, PhD; Carmella Navarro, LPCP; Matthew Orris, MS; Ruby E. Powell, EdD; Lauren Pritchard, MS; Dr. Pat Robey;

Chiquita Kize Rome, MA, NCC, MFP; Ali Sahebi, PhD; and Jean Still, BHsc-Nursing. And finally, Figen Karadogan, PhD, for crunching the numbers on the data collected and committing to write up the research for a presentation at an upcoming conference.

I am also grateful to my beta Mental Freedom coaching groups who trusted me enough to allow me to pilot these ideas with them. Many were already certified in Choice Theory, and their feedback was critical to how the program morphed into what it is today. I will always be grateful to these brave souls who took a chance on me: Sylvester Baugh; Sue Berry; Dr. Scott D'Alerio; Denise Daub, CPT; Bruce Davenport, MA; Elizabeth "Conry" Davidson; Christine Duffield; Amtchat M. Edwards; Osie Harrell; Tony Lamar2; Sheryl F. Matwijkiw; Kathy Randolph, LPC, NCC, CEAP; Maureen Sansom, CTRTC; Pam Slakey, MFT; and Peter Zanol, M. Cath . St, Ba.Ed and Rose Zanol, M.Sp. Path, Ba.Nursing.

I spent a year in Marci Shimoff's "Your Year of Miracles" program to help prepare me for what was to come. I learned to get rid of some limiting beliefs I was holding onto and made some great friends along the way. I am grateful to Marci and her coaches who helped me tremendously: Ally Bird, Beth Larsen, and Cari Garcia.

Coach extraordinaire Paul Iarrobino also helped me immensely when he coached me about a dilemma I was experiencing. He helped me recognize that I could have a greater influence honoring, spreading, and innovating Glasser's ideas outside of William Glasser International (WGI) than I could from inside the organization. It was a painful decision for me to resign my position as executive director so I could be involved full-time with Olver International and Mental Freedom, but I am very happy I did. Of course, I am still a faculty member of WGI, continuing to teach training leading to Choice Theory/Reality Therapy certification, but I no longer have an administrative position, which is great for me. I've never aspired to be an administrator.

I need to acknowledge my gratitude partner, Terri L. Winfree, PhD, for always being supportive and providing a phenomenal location for me to write this book, her timeshare in Cabo, in 2022 and 2024. The energy there is spectacular. I am extremely grateful for our friendship.

I want to thank my peer reviewers who were willing to review one chapter of *Mental Freedom: You Hold the Key* and provide me with their valuable feedback. This book is better because of them: Nessren Ali, MD; Bruce R. Allen, MSW; Francesco Bazzocchi, MEd; Nigel Beckles, CRC, CNAS, PsyRel; Maggie Bolton, CTRTC; Barnes Boffey; Elaine Chung; Leonard Citron, MA, LMHC; Dr. Scott D'Alterio; Bruce Davenport, MS; Richard Doss, PhD; Aleksandra Dzieciolowska-Piatek; Ed Dunkelblau, MA, MEd, PhD; Evisha Ford, LCSW, EdD; Michael Fulkerson, MAE, LPCC-S; Anthony Freire, LMHC, CCMHC; Pam Glasser, MEd; Lacey Glueckert, LAC, MA NCACII; Cynthia Gordon-Wellington, MD, LMHC, LPC, NCC; Diane Gossen, MEd; Mary Amanda Graham, PhD, LMHC; Teresa Greco, OCT, MEd; Kimberly Hambrick, PhD; Monica Hamby, BSN, CRNA; Pam Holtzman; Muriel Soden, MD; Anasuya Jegathevi Jegathesan, PhD; Dr. Figen Karadogan; Joan Karstrom; Dr. Zahra Khoshnevisan; Gigi Kilroe, MD; Vicki Lännerholm, PsyD (ABD), LPCC, LPC, NCC; Rose Lawrence, PhD; Terry Lynch, MD; Rachel McElroy, MS; Wendy Nichols; Janice Ong, MD; Don Parker, EdD; Judy Pedgrift; Timothy Pedigo, PhD; Dr. Ruby Powell; Martin Price, LMHC Dr. Patricia Robey; Jeanette Schneider; Rabbi Shlomo Usher Tauber; Shruti Tekwani, LMHC; Dr. Byron Waller, Gene Wilder, DMin, Dr. Terri Winfree; Marsha Zablotney, NCC, LCP, CAADC, ICAADC, CCDP/D, CTRTC, CCTP, NPT-C, EMDR-PT; Peter and Rose Zanol.

I also want to acknowledge my people. I have a supportive family who allows me to be who I am, and for that, I am extremely grateful: my parents, Carl Daub and Nancy Hankins, have always been in my corner; I have two wonderful brothers, Randy and David Daub; the best two sons a mother could ask for, Dave and Kyle Olver; their beautiful, loving and supportive wives, Stacey and Jesse Olver. My boys and their wives blessed me with eight amazing, intelligent, loving grandchildren: Saige Doreen, Zavier Elias, Logan Thomas, Emerson Naomi, Maeson Amelia, Perry Josephine, Mallory Pearl, and Lincoln Andrew. Every one of my family members has my back and I love them from now into eternity.

I have a spectacular person in my life who deserves mention on her own and that's Denise Daub, my brother Randy's wife. Denise is the backbone of Olver International, my right hand and left brain. I would not have been able to accomplish half of what I have done without her always in the background—supporting, indulging, advising, and sometimes scolding me when I need it. Denise is the sister I never had and the foundation of my business.

I have a wonderful marketing team that started with Denise and branched out to include Marie Hale and her company, @ Revenue. They branded my company Olver International with a name change and a reinvention of my business with a new look, too. Other members of my team include bookkeeper Sheri Macewko; social media manager Joan Karstrom; creative marketer Tina Lee Odensky-Zec, PhD; and newly added marketer and video editor Goran Borojevic. These individuals are gelling to create a beautiful synergy for Olver International and Mental Freedom.

I'd also like to acknowledge the assistance I've received from the Southland Development Authority, the Women's Business Development Center, and the Small Business Association. These organizations stepped up to help small businesses in need during the pandemic and beyond, and I'm very grateful for their assistance.

I have a Mental Freedom team of advisors: Denise Daub, Tony Lamar, and Sylvester Baugh—and the list continues to grow. This is a dream team that is working in lockstep with respect for one another. I couldn't ask for any better.

As for the book, I am always grateful to Denise Daub for creating the cover and doing anything I need from her to make the book launch a success. There's her daughter, my editor since

2016, Veronica Daub, who knows my voice and helps me write more concisely. I love the fantastic job she does editing my work. As you read *Mental Freedom: You Hold the Key*, you have her to thank for the beautiful flow. (She also did the interior design of the book.) I am grateful for Dr. Tina Lee Odensky-Zec's hours of volunteering to help make Mental Freedom's launch a success. I also want to thank Hussein Paymozd, BA for providing the first translation of *Mental Freedom: You Hold the Key* in a foreign language. I hope it is the first of many translations.

Finally, I want to end as I began. Every person I have crossed paths with throughout my life has affected me in some way. I have learned from many people along the way, read countless books, and attended many classes and trainings. I will never be able to mention everyone who has contributed to this book because anyone who has touched my life has had a hand in helping me develop this material. Please forgive me if I have neglected to mention you, but know your influence is indelibly written on my heart. Thank you all!

More Books by Kim Olver

Choosing Me Now

Are you so busy taking care of everyone else in your life that you have forgotten about taking care of yourself? Our focus on creating healthy relationships with others sometimes means we neglect ourselves; the importance of who we are and what we want out of life may get lost. How do you create a healthy relationship with yourself? *Choosing Me Now* teaches how getting to know yourself and learning what satisfies you and your basic needs will help you live a happier and more fulfilling life. (**amzn.to/4bPoQvi**)

Secrets of Happy Couples

Secrets of Happy Couples is different from other books of the same subject because it is based on one basic truth—that all great relationships begin and end with yourself. Any relationship is the sum of its parts: individuals. This book explores how you, as an individual, can make the difference and create a happy and fulfilling relationship with your partner. (**amzn.to/3X7m1Bg**)

Leveraging Diversity at Work

This book helps companies who understand the value of diversity to build, retain, and leverage the diverse workforce they need to be competitive in this country, as well as the global market. The book starts in the very beginning where most books and training programs don't. Before any executive can implement long-term organizational change, the company must ensure the cooperation and conviction of its employees. I am reminded of the saying, "If you think you are leading and no one is following, then you are just out for a walk." (**amzn.to/3RiFF9P**)

A Choice Theory Psychology Guide to Relationships

Do relationships often leave you confused? Do you wonder how two people can be on such different pages most of the time? Do you find it challenging to obtain or maintain meaningful relationships? This book breaks down relationships in an easy-to-understand way, while offering a lot of practical advice on how to improve them. Choice Theory adds a new layer to the topic that is missing from the common knowledge currently known about relationships. (**amzn.to/4bMFqMj**)

What's Happening at Olver International, LLC

Olver International Blog:
olverinternational.com/blog

Life=Choices, Choices-Life Podcast:
life-choices.captivate.fm

Mental Freedom® Programs

Do people or environments sometimes bring you discomfort, anxiety, or frustration? Do you seek emotional empowerment in these situations but aren't sure how to achieve it? The Six Pillars of Mental Freedom® can help. Incorporating the Mental Freedom® OFT framework into your life offers a method to master any circumstance and a pathway toward inner peace. Mental Freedom® is versatile and can be applied to nearly any situation, providing a reliable process to navigate whatever life throws at you. Learn more at olverinternational.com/mental-freedom.

Academy of Choice Coaching® Programs

Our coaching programs at Academy of Choice focus on empowering individuals to take control of their happiness and success by directing their time and energy toward what they can control. We guide people away from blame, anger, and resentment, fostering introspection, acceptance, and proactive behavior. Our approach dismantles the victim mentality, empowering clients to achieve their goals and cultivate meaningful, supportive relationships. Discover more at olverinternational.com/academy-of-choice.

Choice Theory and Reality Therapy Training

Choice Theory® challenges the notion of "misbehavior," suggesting that everyone is simply doing their best to fulfill their needs. While people may break laws, disregard rules, or hurt others in the process, these actions are side effects of their attempts to meet their needs. We believe that everyone is doing their best with the tools and resources available to them. Our training helps individuals develop better tools and behaviors to meet their needs con-structively.

Reality Therapy® complements Choice Theory® by employing a questioning method that skilled counselors use to help clients evaluate the effectiveness of their behavior choices in achieving what they want most. When these behaviors are not working, Reality Therapy® guides clients in making plans to try different approaches, fostering proactive and construc-tive change. Learn more at olverinternational.com/choice-theory-reality-therapy.

InsideOut Press Writers Group

One of the biggest challenges for authors is creating a book that others want to read. Even if your book is exceptional, it must meet industry standards to attract a wider audience beyond just family and friends. Adhering to these standards is crucial for achieving real success. That's where we come in. Join us for a complimentary first session of Writers Group to see if it's for you. For more information, visit freewritersgroup.olverinternational.com

OLVER INTERNATIONAL, LLC
OLVERINTERNATIONAL.COM

Printed in the USA
CPSIA information can be obtained
at www.ICGtesting.com
CBHW021236240624
10562CB00007B/422

9 798985 205435